To Mimi and Dad, GRMA for everything x

A COMPENDIUM OF

IRISH PINTS

THE CULTURE, CUSTOMS AND CRAIC

ALI DUNWORTH

ILLUSTRATED BY STEPHEN HEFFERNAN

NINE BEAN ROWS

CONTENTS

PINTS: AN ORIGIN STORY

In Ireland, a pint – having one, going for one, buying one – is a cultural institution. It's about so much more than 568ml of beer in a glass. But how did a simple pint become such a phenomenon?

It didn't happen overnight. Like all great superheroes, the pint has its own origin story, a long narrative that explains, in part, how our beloved pint culture came into being.

To talk about pints is, of course, to talk about beer. Beer is one of the oldest alcoholic beverages known to humanity. Evidence of its production dates back to 7000 BCE in the ancient civilisations of Egypt, Mesopotamia (modern-day Iraq) and China.

The brewing process itself was likely stumbled upon accidentally during pre-civilisation when we started playing around with agriculture. Maybe some grains were left in water, it was hot and they naturally fermented. Imagine being the first person to have a sip and discover what it did! Initially it was believed that bread was the reason we started domesticating wild grains, but in the 1950s some historians started to think that barley was first domesticated to make ale. It's still debated but I know which side I'm on.

Beer became part of everyday life. It had nutritional value and was a reliable source of hydration, as it was safer to drink than water. It wasn't just practical, though – it eventually became part of social, cultural and religious gatherings, laying the foundations for its enduring popularity that still exist today. Beer is simply an integral part of human history.

In Ireland, we've been fond of a sup for a long time. There is evidence of brewing here that dates back to the Bronze Age and many claim it goes back even further. By medieval times we were brewing even more thanks to the monks, who are thought to have brought back knowledge of brewing from their travels to Rome. Monks took to brewing for sustenance and then for income, and monasteries became the main brewers. The monks were so enamoured of it, they even wrote odes to beer.

They weren't the only holy folks into brewing. One of St Patrick's posse was a monk called Mescan, said to have been his friend and personal brewer. Meanwhile, legend has it that St Brigid, the patron saint of brewing, turned bathwater into beer.

There are too many historical references to alcohol and brewing to go into here but suffice it to say that beer was part of everyday life all over Ireland – not only the drink, but also the drinking.

Beer as nourishment

We've all tried to claim that beer, in particular stout, is good for us at some stage but for a long time it really was thought of as 'liquid nutrition' and was considered to be as important as bread.

People in 15th-century Ireland viewed beer as a healthy, restorative drink. It was unfiltered, made with grains like porridge and was also a good source of calories, so it was the go-to for hardworking labourers. People even believed it could open obstructions in the liver and spleen. It all sounds very compelling but I'm not sure it would hold much sway with today's workforce.

The Brehon Laws and hospitality

It's never just about the drink, though. A big part of why we love pints is the pub and the culture that goes with it. We didn't lick our infamous reputation for hospitality off the ground – it's deeply rooted in our history and it has been ingrained in Irish culture since ancient times.

To understand this part of the origin story we need to go back to the Brehon Laws, our native legal system. These laws were developed from customs that had been passed on orally from one generation to the next before they were written down for the first time in the 7th century AD. They were used right up until the 17th century and governed various parts of Irish life, including land ownership, contracts, marriage, crime and hospitality. The laws were highly detailed and had a big emphasis on hospitality and drinking customs, with references to beer, mead and wine.

Gíall Fóirithne, the Law of Hospitality, dictated that everyone had a moral and legal duty to offer hospitality to all travellers and guests. The Duty of the Host dictated that the host must provide a suitable feast for their guests. 'Beer was the drink of everyday life,' writes Cian Molloy in *The Story of the Irish Pub*. He goes into more detail when he writes about the *Críth Gabhlach*, which states that 'even the lowest grade of freeman should have a cauldron for fermentation in his house with a mug of beer always available for callers'.

The Brehon Laws also have rules around alcohol. For example, it was forbidden to serve weak or diluted drinks during a feast and there were guidelines on the brewing and distribution of ale and mead.

Violating the laws of hospitality was a serious offence. It goes some way towards explaining the significance of sharing a drink in Ireland, including our bonkers obsession with rounds and generosity (see also 'Rounds').

The Brehon Laws have had a huge impact on us as Irish people. Many of our clichéd traits, such as being hospitable and enjoying a drink, are down to the simple fact that we were legally obliged to do these things for a long time. It's no wonder we're so welcoming.

The invaders

A good origin story needs hardships or a nemesis and Ireland had plenty. The Anglo-Norman invasion of Ireland in the 12th century brought big changes to the country, including changes to our drinking habits. Towns and urban areas were established with new trading centres and taverns began to appear. Of course, they wanted to tax the booze. This was probably the first sign of alcohol licensing in Ireland and the beginning of the Irish pub. As roads and infrastructure developed, more inns and lodgings for travellers opened that served food and with that, of course, beer.

Over the following centuries the English settled in, leaving an indelible mark on the country. Their regulations and bureaucracy imposed new legal standards around pub operations and taxes. Permits and licensing laws appeared, resulting in a greater flow of financial resources directed towards the English administration in Ireland. The look and feel of the taverns changed too. They started to turn into the pubs we know today. The English pub-style architecture started to appear, with timber frames, thatched roofs and a distinct layout.

As we move to the 20th century, we had pubs everywhere and battles to be fought. Much has been written about the pub's role in the Irish struggle for freedom. It's well documented that many were used in Irish rebellions as meeting places, for planning, to store weapons, as places of ambush and places to spy – so much so that historian Eddie Bohan wrote a book on the subject called *Thirst for Freedom*. He describes how pubs were used for good at first but also how drinking hindered much of the planning – basically, drunk revolutionaries were no use.

Even though drinking was shunned by the cause, pubs still played an important role. Publicans and bar staff were often the most in the know and connected people in the community, which was ideal for helping to spread word or warning when needed. During the 1916 Rising in Dublin, the Irish rebels seized pubs because of their location as they were often on corners, overlooking main roads. They used distilleries too because the chimneys were good viewing points.

Temperance and shebeens

Started by a Catholic priest, Theobald Mathew, in the early 19th century, the Irish Temperance movement was dedicated to reducing the consumption of alcohol in Ireland and addressing the perceived social issues associated with alcohol. It gained momentum over the next century and gathered support from both Protestant and Catholic religious leaders and politicians, resulting in the subsequent introduction of strict licensing laws in the late 19th and early 20th centuries.

Meanwhile, across the pond, the US also decided to turn its back on drinking, although they took it much further. In 1920 they introduced Prohibition, a complete ban on alcohol and hard liquor, in an attempt to save the nation and banish the evils associated with alcohol.

A complete ban didn't happen in Ireland but laws imposed limitations on pub opening hours and the sale of alcohol. In both cases, an important point was forgotten: we like to drink! And as soon as you slap restrictions on things people like, we will find a way around them.

The Americans created their now infamous speakeasies, while in Ireland we returned to an old favourite: the shebeen. Shebeens were not a new concept. They'd been a part of Ireland ever since booze had been taxed, but this time there was a resurgence of makeshift 'pubs' and venues in back rooms in private houses or hidden-away sheds – anywhere you thought a clandestine gathering would be safe from prying eyes.

The thing is, it wasn't just about the booze. It was about socialising on your own terms, without being told when to go home and without restrictions. The more alcohol was pushed as a social taboo, the more appealing it became to sneak off for a drink. There was devilment and secrecy around having a drink. The drink became more than its contents, more than its glass.

Eventually, as licensing laws and attitudes towards alcohol changed, shebeens began to dissipate but the term 'shebeen' lives on in some pub names. The word still has a certain meaning and implication that gives you that giddy feeling. It's no surprise we saw a resurgence of shebeens and home pubs during the covid lockdowns in 2020 and 2021.

So between beer's strong start as a nutritious staple, the enduring effect the Brehon Laws have had on Ireland and the struggles the Irish and our pubs have had to overcome, it's no wonder that when we talk about a pint or going for a pint, it means so much more than the contents of a glass..

AFTER-WORK PINTS

Unwinding after work with a drink, shaking off the day and the shackles, getting to have some unstructured time with your colleagues to build camaraderie or bitch about your boss – few things taste better than that well-earned after-work pint, so it's no wonder drinking after (and sometimes during!) work has been part of human culture in various forms for a long time.

A short history of after-work pints

The practice of a post-workday pint in a pub kicked off around the Industrial Revolution. As Ireland became more urban and industrial work increased, people gathered at pubs or taverns after working on the docks or in a mill (*people* predominantly being male, which was a factor in how the pub was traditionally the preserve of men – see also 'The old man's pub' for more on this). Alcohol began its infamous relationship with the after-work crowd and after-work drinks eventually became a staple ritual to separate work from play.

In Kingsley Amis's book *On Drink*, he writes about the rapid increase in drinking in urban cultures:

❝ The strains and stresses of urban living, to coin a phrase, are usually held accountable for these increases ... sudden confrontation with complete or comparative strangers in circumstances requiring a show of relaxation and amiability ... the reason why I, and most others, usually turn out to enjoy meeting such creatures is simply and obviously the co-presence of drink.

9-5

5-9

The three types of after-work pints

After-work pints can differ depending on the type of job you have but in general there are three main types of situation you are likely to encounter when you swap the swivel chair for the bar stool.

....

The swiftie When you genuinely go for just the one (see also pages 112–14). You have one pint that quenches your thirst and marks the end of the day and the start of the evening (or even better, the weekend). You have a nice brief chat with your work friends, then you head off. This after-work pint tends to be a bit of a unicorn, though. Calling it after one pint is not a skill that everyone has in them.

....

The proper pints This is the sweet spot. It may be an occasion, a birthday, a leaving do or just a Friday or sunny midweek evening, but whatever it is there's a reason you should stay for more than one. Bonus if someone's there with a company card buying the drinks. You get the polite chat out of the way and then you get a bit more into it. You end up sitting beside your work bestie or someone you've wanted to have a gossip or a chat with or maybe even someone you fancy. The pints and the chats flow. When the proper pints go well, you've bonded, you've laughed, you've had a good time. Ideally you don't say anything too inappropriate or overshare. This is after-work pint perfection.

....

The one too many (oh no, what did I do/say?) It started out as proper pints. Things were going well but you or someone else got carried away. There was that extra pint you said you didn't need, someone ordered shots or maybe you were deep in a bitching session and didn't want to leave. Whatever the reason, if you've been there, you know – and you may still even have the fear (see also page 102) about whatever happened or was said. Let there be solace in knowing you are not alone. The less said about the one-too-many-after-work drinks, the better.

After-work pints in the hospitality industry

Anyone who works in hospitality has another take on after-work pints because they have their pints when we're all at home in bed or recovering from the night before. Irish chef Christine Walsh describes the magic of off-duty chef pints perfectly:

❝ Picture this. You've worked for 10 hours straight. You're annoyed, exhausted and fed up. You're off tomorrow but no plans are made. Half an hour to finish and your mate texts, 'Pint?' It's one of the best feelings – giddiness, excitement, knowing you can go and sit in a pub, no rush on anyone, have talks and laughs and just completely decompress for a few hours in the company of the people you're most comfortable being around before going home.

My favourite type of pint is on a Sunday afternoon, when all the messy arseholes from Saturday nights have crawled home in bits. Sundays are left with the best people out just wanting slow, happy, drama-free pints.

Going for pints is not about getting pissed. It's the social, banter-loving atmosphere that we crave the most with the people we like the most.

AIRPORT PINTS

There is an unwritten rule once you pass airport security that you are in no man's land when it comes to time, which means having a drink is acceptable – and often encouraged – at any time of the day. It's always five o'clock somewhere when you're in a departure lounge.

Dublin Airport is a particularly good example of this, with Terminal 1 leading the way. Even if you arrive bleary-eyed in the wee hours, someone will be drinking a pint. At busy times there's a palpable buzz that only adds to the excitement if you're heading off.

For many, the airport pint is a holiday tradition. They plan to get there early, meet with friends and catch up. It's the ultimate klaxon to say, right, I'm switched off and holiday mode is on.

You might spot groups in matching tracksuits with 'Team Bride' emblazoned on the back tucking into drinks before they board their Ryanair flights to Spain or rowdy gangs in matching T-shirts proclaiming their tribe (Johnno's Stag! Mary's 50th!) en route to Liverpool or Vegas.

....

In the 1950s, the Dublin Airport restaurant was *the* place to be. It was a chic, linen tablecloth affair. People with no intention of ever flying would get dressed up and head there for the evening. Dances were even held there. No doubt a few bottles of porter were drunk. It's no wonder there's still a sense of devilment in the air when you get there.

....

OUT OF OFFICE

Non-drinking travellers look on and laugh (mostly) and business travellers pretend to ignore them and tap on their laptops. Couples heading off without their kids (yay!) order a drink, looking forward to the undisturbed sleep as much as the sunshine. Solo travellers sip away and enjoy the unrivalled people-watching an airport offers. Then there are the travellers who are leaving Ireland for a while, cherishing what might be their last decent pint until they return.

Whatever the reason, the airport pint is unique and the camaraderie in Irish airport bars is something not seen elsewhere.

And it's become a ubiquitous social media post. You'd think you can't get on a flight without uploading a 'pint and passport' picture along with a cheesy caption like 'Out of office is on!' Guinness has cottoned on (as they usually do) that there's quite the demand for a perfect pint of the black stuff before people head off and in 2022 opened a dedicated Guinness bar in Dublin Airport's Terminal 1. It's a fine pour there and it's hard to resist a quick stop if you've got 20 minutes to spare.

If you're not an airport pinter, why not? Next time you fly, try it for yourself – just don't forget your 'out of office' social media post.

BAD PINTS

> ❝ If a good pint is a godly gift, a bad pint is an abomination, an affront to humanity. **(Dublin Pub Life and Lore by Kevin C. Kearns)**

It's a travesty when you're looking forward to a pint and it doesn't deliver. But not all bad pints are created equally bad.

The badly poured pint

You get served a badly poured pint. Maybe there's some drink dripping down the side of the glass. Perhaps the glass is dirty or there's lipstick on the rim. Maybe it's been poured into the wrong glass (see also 'The pint glass'). Perhaps the head is too big ('Is the Pope in town?') or there's no head at all. It's flatter than you expected or bubblier than you're used to.

The non-pint drinker may consider these superficial slights. It's still beer, right? It's still got booze in it. It will still do the job. But pint drinkers, we're a particular bunch. We want our pints served a certain way, and when they're not, well, we tend to get quite het up about it. Nothing encapsulates this better than the phenomenon of an Instagram account called Shit London Guinness.

Shit London Guinness

In 2019, Ian Ryan, a Cork man living in London, became frustrated by the quality of some of the pints he was getting served in the capital. To vent said frustrations he set up an account to document the shit pints he was served. The bio reads: 'Documenting all of the shite pints of Guinness in London. For my sins.'

SPILLED

your GUIDE to SHIT PINTS OF GUINNESS

TINY HEAD

HUGE HEAD

BUBBLY?

WRONG GLASS

NO HEAD AT ALL

LOOKS FINE, TASTES LIKE SHITE

Ryan was not alone in his dismay. The shit pints he shared struck a chord with much of the Irish diaspora in the UK and further afield. Finally, there was someone to turn to when you were served a bad pint. Pint drinkers lapped it up and the account went viral. At the time of writing, Ryan has almost a quarter of a million followers. It's no wonder – we know outrage brings engagement, and a lot of people are outraged by the tragic-looking specimens shoddily poured into inappropriate glassware, with dribbly sides or ridiculous heads on them. Sure, giving out about bad pints is practically a national pastime for pint drinkers.

But the pints haven't been all shit for Ryan. His Instagram account has been mentioned on Graham Norton's show by Jamie Dornan, he sells Shit London Guinness merch and he's even written a book, *A Beautiful Pint: One Man's Search for the Perfect Pint of Guinness*.

The 'bad pint'

Ah, the 'bad pint'. We've all claimed to have had one of these. Those sneaky 'bad pints' you didn't even realise you've had. You know the ones I'm talking about.

When you have that inexplicable hangover you don't think reflects the night before? Bad pint!

When you're late for work and they know you were out but you swear you only had a few? Bad pint!

When you told your boss/colleague/friend/person you fancy what you really think of them but don't remember? Bad pint!

It's been wheeled out as a wondrous excuse and has shouldered the blame for too much exuberance on many occasions. Cheers to the 'bad pint'!

The actual bad pint

The pint you know is off straightaway, and not just superficially. To be fair, most Irish people drink the same pints for years, if not decades, so we get to know our tipple fairly well. When we're poured a pint that just doesn't feel right, we trust our gut. It might be a bit more obvious, like it's flat or overexcited or the colour is off. But you can also tell by taste and smell. You just know when it's not right.

It shouldn't be a common occurrence with the commercial drinks we're so fond of, particularly Guinness, who take great pride in their quality control. But there's always human error. Shit happens and sometimes a pint is bad.

There are a few main things people blame the bad pint on (even if they have never poured a pint in their life): a dirty glass (not just superficially), residue on the glass, a 'bad' keg, a cellar that's too warm, a cellar that's too cold, not enough gas, too little gas, the wrong gas and so on. A pint 'expert' who claims to know more than the bar staff could have even more insights (see also 'Experts on pints').

Glasses are fair game. If a pub isn't looking after their glasses properly, well, they're not looking after us properly. Some pubs even have a separate glass washer just for Guinness glasses. Nothing else goes in there, not even detergent, just lovely hot water. This ensures the glasses are never adulterated and the 'schtick' sticks as it should. Badly treated glasses can definitely be blamed for a bad pint.

In addition, the lines get blamed for many a hiccup. The lines are the hard-working tubes that get your beer from the keg in the cellar up to the bar tap. Stout drinkers in particular love to discuss the lines, citing optimum lengths of line from keg to bar and how that affects your pint.

But when we're blaming lines for bad pints, we're usually talking about cleaning the lines. These days the beer suppliers tend to clean the lines in the pubs as needed so it shouldn't be an issue, but back when bar staff were the ones responsible for doing this task in-house, I'm sure there were hiccups that could have resulted in a few bad pints. How do I know? Because I worked in pubs back when we cleaned the lines in-house...

Bad pint etiquette

What do you do when you get a bad pint? Do you:

A Exercise your rights as a customer and bring it back to be exchanged
B Drink it anyway and give out about it the entire time
C Don't drink it, leave the pub and never darken their doors again
D Take a picture and post it on Instagram

We know we should choose Option A but we don't do this as often as we should. Maybe you're in a round and it's too much hassle. Maybe the bar person is just handing out shit pints so you don't bother. Maybe the alcohol is more important than the pint itself. There are a myriad of reasons we put up and shut up, but we shouldn't. Dear reader, if you do get a bad pint, please return it!

BEER MATS

There are many things around pint drinking that are just instinctive, expected, unspoken. Beer mats are one of these things. If you're drinking a pint, you expect there to be a beer mat under it. In Ireland, at least.

This was a culture shock when I moved to the UK in my early twenties. I can still recall the sloppiness of the tables with the pint glasses dripping, little spills and condensation with nowhere to go except the dark wood table gathering in a sticky wet mess ready to ruin your sleeves. Yuck.

Not so in Ireland. I walked into a pub just the other day and every single round table had exactly four beer mats laid out, ready for the drinks that were to come. At the bar, beer mats were placed helpfully by the taps so the bar person could put one under your pint before it landed in front of you. Or you can grab a few for the table just in case. As a pint drinker, it's a natural instinct to always make sure there is a beer mat. We are not animals.

I want a proper beer mat with my pint. The cardboard kind, not a reusable chunky one and certainly not a napkin. I can just about put up with the posh white paper ones with an embossed logo in a hotel, but mostly I want a proper pub beer mat. And I want it to correspond with my pint. If I'm drinking Guinness, I'd prefer a Guinness beer mat. It's not essential, but it's pleasing for it all to work together.

In a world where we strive to be more sustainable and environmentally friendly, you would think that these low-usage pieces of cardboard might have been demonised but not in Ireland. It seems we value dry tables and sleeves more than reducing our carbon footprint.

But beer mats do so much more than just keep our tables drip-free. They have had multiple uses over the years.

Beer mats are brilliant marketing tools. Big brands will supply pubs with boxes of them so that their logo is what you see on the table. I've heard rumours that there are even supposed beer mat contracts with pubs, where pubs will have agreed to use only particular branded beer mats at certain times of the year.

Beer mat advertising spaces have been sold to all sorts of businesses, not just beers. Taxi companies are obvious ones. Various government campaigns have even been seen on them.

Pubs do their own branded beer mats too. They look smart and can tell you a bit about the pub. The Gravediggers in Dublin is a perfect example of this. Their beer mat message is simple and impactful: 'Est 1833. Proudly owned and run by the 6th, 7th and 8th Generation of the Kavanagh Family.' And of course they include the links for all their social media and their own hashtag #heaveninglasnevin. No doubt many of these have been pocketed and taken to homes all over the world and have encouraged pint drinkers to share a snap on their own socials.

Beer mats weren't just for brands and pubs to communicate to us – we used them for our own purposes too. When you went to the pub before mobile phones and met someone, you wrote your number on a beer mat. When you had a great idea or wanted to remember something before we had the Notes app on our phones, you could jot it down on a beer mat. Creative types in particular could often be seen scribbling on a beer mat when something came to them. The late, great Shane McGowan was a fan of writing lyrics on a beer mat, according to his wife.

When you're debating what should have happened in a football game you watched or played, beer mats become the players on the field and the table becomes the pitch so you can explain your expert logic to your pals.

The fidgety among us are always grateful for something in our hands to play with, from balancing the beer mats or making a little building to flipping it off the side of the table and catching it. But one person's nervous fidgeting is most people's annoyance. If someone asks you to stop, you stop. The one fidgeting I can't condone, though, is peeling a beer mat. We've all seen someone do it − picking off bits of cardboard and making a little pile on the table. Just don't. No one likes it, especially the bar staff.

Another important role of the beer mat is that of the seat saver. If you're drinking your pint and have to nip to the loo or outside for a smoke, you just pop a beer mat on top of your pint and everyone knows not to touch it, that you will be back momentarily.

THE 8TH WONDER

BIRTHDAY PINTS

I got a birthday card once that said, 'You know what rhymes with birthday? Pints!' It's spot on.

It doesn't even have to be your own birthday – anyone's birthday is a good excuse for pints. Pints for your birthday are the failproof, safe bet for no stress for the birthday person and the invitees.

Birthday pints are so much easier than any other social birthday situation. Birthday dinner? No, thanks! If there are more than six people, you won't get a good table. You'll have to order off a set menu. You won't get to talk to everyone who has come. There will be awkward balloons hitting someone in the face. Do you bring your own cake? And if so, will you get charged cakeage? (Yes, that's a thing now.) And then the bill comes. Who's going to split it? Ugh. You should have just gone for pints.

The same goes for any organised birthday outing – all that planning and booking things, confirming, buying tickets and transferring money. You know what needs very little forward planning and very little work on the night? Birthday pints.

All it takes is a text message or similar. Pints, a time and a place. That's it! Everyone knows what to expect. You'll meet up, have pints, talk shit and laugh a lot. Some will go home when they should and some might go dancing or to the chipper (see also 'The chipper and pints'). All in all it should be a stress-free night, although that entirely depends on you and your mates. The same goes for the hangover the next day.

BRAND LOYALTY

It was only after I moved to London in my early twenties that I realised we are super brand loyal when it comes to pints in Ireland. Not only would I walk into bars and see taps I didn't recognise, but most surprising of all, I'd see different sets of taps in every pub.

It was a shock to the system not to see the usual repertoire of Guinness, Smithwick's, Heineken, Carlsberg, Bulmers, et al. I had to learn to switch my pint to suit my pub and realised most people just asked for lager, no preference.

I know now that the business model for pubs in the UK is different than it is here. A lot of pubs there are 'tied houses', which means they might be owned by a brewery and therefore have to sell that brewery's beers, so that can limit options. There is also a lot more real ale available in the UK and Guinness isn't standard everywhere (although that's changing).

Now I'm not saying it's necessarily a good thing that Irish pubs have traditionally offered the same beers on tap in every pub – monopolies are not known to be good for consumers. Yet there's a certain comfort in knowing 'your' pint is available, not to mention knowing how it will taste, how boozy it will be and how much it will cost.

Things have started to change a bit in Ireland, with craft beers appearing more often (see also 'Craft beer'). I wonder if we will be just as brand loyal with them?

CAMRA (the Campaign for Real Ale) in the UK promotes and advocates having quality real ale, cider and perry in pouring and thriving pubs in every community. It was set up in 1971 by four beer enthusiasts but guess what their push to do so was? A visit to Ireland.

Speaking on the CAMRA podcast Pubs. Pints. People, founder Bill Mellor spoke about how it happened and the pint of 'ale' that drove them to it:

> **❝** On our travel through Ireland we were repeatedly lamenting the state of British beer and indeed Irish beer apart from Guinness and a couple of other stouts. The most ubiquitous so-called beer was a dreadful-tasting concoction called Smithwick's, which was very similar to the Double Diamond and Whitbread we were drinking in England. We decided something needed to be done and came up with the idea for CAMRA. Now where did we make this momentous decision to form CAMRA? It was far west of County Kerry, to the most westerly point of Ireland, which is a place called Kruger's Bar at the tip of the Dingle Peninsula.

Considering our unwavering brand loyalty over the years, it would be remiss not to list some of the favourites, the most memorable, the nostalgic pints, the traditional pints, the forgotten pints and some of the pints we'd like to forget.

STOUT
Guinness
Guinness is often touted as Ireland's national drink. I've read claims that a pint of Guinness is more easily recognised around the world as Irish than our tricolour national flag. Quite simply, it is intrinsically linked with Ireland, so it's no surprise that when we talk about pints, going for pints or

having a pint, most of us will automatically picture a pint of Guinness. In fact, there are still many bars in Ireland where when you walk in and simply ask for a pint with no more specifics, you will be poured a pint of Guinness.

Guinness is the original, the leader of the pack, the go-to, the archetypal drink poured in a pint glass in Ireland. But what is it that we're actually pouring and drinking?

For the most part, we're talking about Guinness Draught, which is made of water, malted and roasted barley, hops, yeast and nitrogen. The water is not from the River Liffey, as is sometimes claimed – Guinness actually uses water from the Wicklow Mountains. The malted barley, they say, forms the foundation of the Guinness and the dark-roasted barley is what gives it its distinctive rich taste and dark, ruby-red hue. The hops combine with the roasted barley to balance out the flavour.

As for the yeast, they use their own Guinness yeast, a strain they say has been handed down for generations. Apparently a reserve amount is kept under lock and key just in case anything should happen to the main supply. And of course nitrogen is an

'Look closely. Guinness Draught beer is not actually black but rather dark ruby red because of the way the ingredients are prepared. Some raw barley is roasted, in a similar way to coffee beans, which is what gives Guinness Draught its distinctive colour.' (guinness.com)

essential part of the surge, settle and creamy head we've come to expect from every pint.

Then there are the ingredients you can't list: the myth, lore, marketing and history that have led to Guinness having an indelible place in the hearts of Irish pint drinkers (see also 'Guinness: A pint-sized history').

GUINNESS COMBOS

....

Black velvet This Guinness–Champagne combination was created in 1861 by a bartender at Brooks's Club in London to honour the death of Albert, the Prince Consort of Queen Victoria, because he thought even a glass of bubbly should be in mourning and dressed in black.

....

Guinness and blackcurrant A classic combo – a pint of Guinness with a dash of blackcurrant cordial thrown in.

....

Pint of special A pint of Smithwick's topped up with Guinness or variations thereof. This one tastes good.

....

Black and Tan Something the (usually American) internet gets very wrong is that a Black and Tan is a popular drink in Ireland. It's not, and with good reason. While we may enjoy mixing black (stout) and tan (pale ale) beers in a pint of special (see above), we certainly don't embrace naming a drink this. The Black and Tans was what we called the British paramilitary force formed to suppress the Irish War of Independence in the 1920s. So as you can imagine, we are not the biggest fans and definitely don't want a drink named after them. Best not to order this one. (Although not a pint, the same thing goes for the shot called an Irish car bomb. Just don't.)

....

Murphy's

Cork certainly lives up to its 'Rebel County' name when it comes to stout – it's probably the only place in Ireland where you're not guaranteed to find Guinness on tap in the pub. Murphy's is the stout that reigns supreme in Cork, closely followed by Beamish (more on that below).

Murphy's has been brewed in Cork since the 1850s, when James J. Murphy and his brothers sold their shares in the Midleton Distillery to found the Lady's Well Brewery on Leitrim Street in Cork City. Murphy guided the brewery to success and by the 1860s it had established itself as one of the major breweries in the country. In the 1880s they expanded the business and began producing Murphy's Stout. It was stronger than porter and is said to have been a 'generous and pleasant drink' (Ó Drisceoil and Ó Drisceoil, 1997).

There are many parallels to Guinness besides them both being Irish stouts. James Murphy was not unlike Arthur Guinness in giving back to the city he brewed in – Murphy was a noted philanthropist in Cork. There were parallels with the stouts too. Murphy's was also touted as a health giver. *The Murphy's Story: The History of Lady's Well Brewery, Cork* by Diarmuid Ó Drisceoil and Donal Ó Drisceoil gives us a good few descriptions of the stout at this time. They tell us the brewery was 'not averse to promoting the medicinal value of its brews'. A visitors' guide to the brewery published in 1902 stated that 'porter is acknowledged by the medical profession to be a most nourishing drink when taken in moderation' and 'we also tested some invalid stout, a beverage highly recommended by doctors for its powerful tonic properties, and for which the firm is famous'.

The Murphy's logo is the Murphy family coat of arms and the motto is *Fortis et Hospitalis*, which means 'strength and hospitality' – fitting for a stout brand.

In the 1970s the company merged with Beamish & Crawford, which gave it more of a presence in the stout market. Heineken bought the Murphy's brand in 1983, which meant Murphy's Irish Stout was introduced to international markets and is now exported globally.

Still, there's no getting away from competing with Guinness; it's like having a very popular older sibling. But it's a fact they don't shy away from. On Murphy's US website they call themselves 'the People's Pint' and say, 'We challenge the everyday pint and proudly champion a simply crafted stout.' I think we all know what that 'everyday pint' is.

....

Before James Murphy established his brewery he was involved in running the Midleton Distillery, which had been founded by his relatives. He sold his share of the distillery to fund setting up the brewery. This distillery later became Irish Distillers, which is now one of the greatest success stories of the Irish drinks industry. It's the largest distiller of Irish whiskey, distilling popular brands such as Jameson and Powers in addition to premium whiskeys such as Redbreast and Midleton Very Rare.

....

Beamish

In Cork you will find many pubs where the go-to pint is a 'Creamy Beamy', or Beamish to the rest of us. It's a stout beloved by Corkonians with origins dating back to 1792, when the brewery was established as the Cork Porter Brewery by philanthropists William Beamish and William Crawford. The brewery's founding families played a huge role in Cork's cultural life so there is a lot of goodwill associated with Beamish, much like Guinness and its reputation of looking after Dubliners.

Before Guinness was the drink of choice in Ireland, Beamish led the way. In 1805, it was the largest brewery in Ireland and the third largest in Britain and Ireland. It held the title of being the largest Irish brewery until it was overtaken by Guinness in 1833.

Beamish was a local business until 1962, when Canadian brewing firm Carling-O'Keefe bought the brewery. It changed hands again in 1995 to Scottish & Newcastle, which meant the brewery was then owned by Heineken. But much like Guinness, which is now owned by global giant Diageo, the goodwill garnered by years of looking after their own has never gone away, so Cork people are still smitten with Beamish.

More recently, Beamish has had a bit of a renaissance as stout continues to be a popular choice for the young hipsters of Ireland. Pairing Beamish with your rollies could be considered to be just a little bit cooler and quirkier than Guinness. There's also the fact that it's usually a bit cheaper too. And don't forget it's creamy! Cheers to Creamy Beamy.

LAGER
Budweiser
We're talking about US Budweiser here, the (self-proclaimed) King of Beers, not to be confused with Budweiser Budvar (see below). Both beers entered the Irish market in the 1980s but the US Budweiser made the most impact, probably thanks in part to Guinness (Diageo) not only brewing Budweiser in Ireland under licence but also marketing and distributing their beers. That's hard to compete with.

The US version had the edge even before that, though. Budweiser arrived in Ireland at a time when all things American were coveted here and Budweiser was synonymous with American culture. I started drinking in the 1990s and Budweiser was what I started on. It ticked all the boxes: it was marketed as just beer, nothing complicated; I thought it was cool; and probably most importantly, it didn't really taste of much.

It was a short-lived affair. By the time they launched their infamous 'Whassup?' advertising campaign in 1999, I'd moved on – and eventually, so did most Irish drinkers. You won't find Budweiser on tap in many pubs these days. It's usually been replaced by Coors (see below).

Budvar

The ongoing *Budweiser v. Budvar* legal dispute involves two beer companies: the American company known for Budweiser and the Czech firm Budějovický Budvar, both of which have been selling beer under the name 'Budweiser' since the late 19th century.

In some countries Budvar is imported as Czechvar. In Ireland, even though they can technically call it Budweiser Budvar, it's most commonly called Budvar. It's a different beer to US Budweiser, which is your typical American-style beer, whereas Budweiser Budvar is a Continental lager.

We went mad for Budvar in the late 1990s and early 2000s, when we decided Czech beer was sophisticated. It's still around – maybe not on tap in many places – and it's still a solid choice.

Carlsberg

Probably the best at marketing themselves after Guinness. Love them or hate them, we all know the Carlsberg 'probably' ads. They've been around for years and have been parodied for just as long. They've even won marketing awards for the campaigns. Yet Carlsberg has never felt as premium as Heineken (if you could call either premium, that is).

In my early years of pints, I quickly moved from Budweiser to Carlsberg. I don't remember why but I do remember it tasted more of 'beer' than the soapy pints of Budweiser had, and I drank it as 'my' pint for many years.

They've had a few rebrands over the years. These days it's pitched as 'Danish pilsner', no doubt an attempt to piggyback on the superstardom of Danish cuisine but I don't think it'll be gaining Noma-style stardom anytime soon. Still, Carlsberg has always done okay in Ireland although I'd say that owes more to the fact that it's brewed here by Diageo, and therefore you'll find it in most Guinness pubs, than its own kudos. Probably.

Coors

Coors (formerly known as Coors Light) arrived on tap in Ireland in the early 2000s after already making quite an impact with its all-American bottled beer. They simply marketed it as cold and refreshing, promising beer 'as cold as the Rockies'.

But it wasn't the coldness that caught our attention in Ireland. The word 'light' in the name added to its appeal, especially to women (at the start, anyway), although it wasn't always clear if it was lighter in booze or in calories. It simply claimed to have 'fewer calories and less alcohol per serving' – than what, though?

It didn't seem to matter. The ladies took a liking to it, so much so that it was the original drink of choice for Aisling in the *Oh My God What a Complete Aisling* series of books. Aisling is a fictional character created by Emer McLysaght and Sarah Breen who perfectly encapsulates an archetypal Irish girl. We all either know an Aisling or *are* an Aisling. On the original Facebook page that the books are based on, the authors write:

❝ She's your stereotypical friend who carries her court shoes to work in a bag while pounding the pavement with her MBTs on the walk in from Rathmines. Aisling loves a Colours Night in the Portobello and a cheeky Coors Light in McGowans of Phibsboro. She keeps all of her Laser receipts and checks them off against her bank statement. She has a loyalty card from both Tesco and Dunnes but not Marks & Spencer, have you seen the prices in there? Aisling loves a good bit of drying and thinks tumble driers are a sinful waste.

Coors Light has many other Irish celebrity fans, including Michael Flatley of *Riverdance* fame. According to a news story in the *Irish Daily Mail* on 20 September 2013, he celebrated his birthday in a Kerry pub where publican John C. O'Shea was quoted as saying, 'He was delighted to buy a round and he enjoyed a few Coors Light himself. He said he finds the Guinness a bit heavy.'

Singer Mary Byrne loves a few pints too and lamented her love of Coors Light in the news before she embarked on RTÉ's *Operation Transformation* in 2017, saying, 'I've a terrible habit eating crisps and I love my pint of Coors Light at the weekend. I don't have just one, I have about five or six.'

Foster's

Another fairly unremarkable beer with excellent branding, Foster's describes itself as a lager with a 'bright golden colour that delivers a refreshing beer-drinking experience with a crisp-clean hop finish'. First brewed in Australia in 1887, it arrived on Irish shores in the mid-1980s with advertising featuring one of our favourite Aussies, Paul Hogan (aka Crocodile Dundee), and the tagline 'Australian for beer!'

It was a popular tap for a while but it didn't ever win us over properly. These days, as more and more Irish people spend time living and working in Australia, we've realised that there is much more to Aussie beer than this 'Amber Nectar'. However, it will forever be remembered by anyone who went to university in Ireland in the late 1990s and early 2000s, when the brand ran a lot of student-focused promotions, including handing out Foster's 'dollars' that could be exchanged for pints, while at least one university bar I know of had a loyalty card scheme for pints of Foster's where you bought three and got the fourth free.

Foster's may call itself 'the Australian for lager' but it's not all brewed in Australia. The Foster's sold in Ireland comes from Manchester. In 2015, a New York man sued the United States brewers of the famous export because he claimed he was given the false impression it was made in Australia.

Mineken

Harp

The smell of Harp is the smell of the pub in the 1990s, along with smoking indoors, sticky bars and carpets. It was created by Guinness in 1960, when Continental lagers started to become popular in Ireland and the UK. Harp was the go-to lager in Irish pubs for a long time but it had a tough time competing with the newer names as they appeared in pubs in the 1990s and 2000s. It didn't help that it was saddled with the nickname 'Harpic' (after a popular bleach brand), which was immortalised when Christy Moore used it in the lyrics for his song 'Delirium Tremens'. He mentions a few others but none fare as badly as poor Harp:

> Goodbye to the port and brandy, to the vodka and the Stag,
> To the Schmiddick and the Harpic, the bottled draught and keg.
> As I sat lookin' up the Guinness ad I could never figure out
> How your man stayed up on the surfboard after fourteen pints of stout.

In Northern Ireland, however, Harp has remained a popular choice. More recently, I've seen Harp taps appearing again around the rest of Ireland. With the 1990s back in fashion, is Harp due a revival?

Heineken

Heineken has done very well for itself in Ireland since Murphy's Brewery in Cork launched the beer in 1978. The global brewer then went on to buy out the Murphy's Brewery and now the Heineken brewery in Cork is where they're talking about when they say they brew 'over 98% of our draught beer sold in Ireland'.

Ireland has a lot of love for this Dutch lager, which is consistently touted as the most popular drink of choice for lager drinkers in Ireland. I think it does well because it's an all-rounder. It's probably the most beige lager of the lot, and I'm not talking about the colour. It doesn't taste too much of anything, it's refreshing and it's not too boozy (4.3% ABV). The consistency with which it has sponsored sports in Ireland has to have had an effect too (see also 'Sports and pints'). More recently, music festival sponsorship has been another big one.

Ireland's most famous Heineken drinker has to be Ross O'Carroll Kelly, a fictional creation of writer Paul Howard. Ross is a rugby-obsessed, obnoxious southside Dubliner who famously drinks 'Heino'. Over hundreds of *Irish Times* columns and 26 books, Howard has satirised Irish rugby fans via O'Carroll Kelly, who is never far from a pint of Heino, often drinking them in his favourite (now no more) pub, Kiely's of Donnybrook.

In the original iteration of Ross O'Carroll Kelly that appeared in the *Sunday Tribune* sports section before he moved to the *Irish Times*, Ross drank Miller, not Heineken! Wonder what the *goys* think of that?

Heino isn't the only nickname the beer has garnered over the years. It's also called:

- Pint of Ken
- Heino
- Heiny
- Heinomite
- Two sticks of Heinomite
- Vitamin H
- The Leinster Handcuffs
- Green Grenade (usually referring to a bottle)

RED ALE
Smithwick's

Dating back to at least 1710, Smithwick's is likely Ireland's oldest beer brand, best known for its much-loved red ale. It was founded by John Smithwick at St Francis's Abbey Brewery in Kilkenny City, where the Franciscan monks would likely have been distilling and brewing beer long before then.

John Smithwick was a Catholic, which meant that under the penal laws of the time he wasn't allowed to own property or run for elected office. So he went into business with Protestant Richard Cole on a piece of land that Cole had leased from the Duke of Ormond, who lived in Kilkenny Castle, in 1705.

Smithwick ran the business successfully and kept a low profile for decades until the repeal of the penal laws in the late 1700s, when he could rightly take his place in Kilkenny society. By 1827 the Smithwick name was proudly displayed over the gate.

Over the years, Smithwick's Brewery expanded its operations and developed a loyal following in Ireland. In 1964, Guinness bought a controlling share in the business, which later became Diageo. In 1965, the brewery ceased production in Kilkenny and relocated to the Guinness brewery in Dublin. It was good timing, as Guinness had just nailed their own Guinness Draught and thus used their know-how to launch Smithwick's Draught Ale in 1966, which is pretty much the same pint that's still poured today.

DID YOU KNOW?
John Smithwick was good friends with one of the great Irish politicians of the 19th century, 'The Liberator' Daniel O'Connell.

CIDER

Bulmers

If you think there has been a monopoly on Irish beers, cider in Ireland has it even worse. For a long time, a singular brand dominated and probably still does: Bulmers (or Magners as it's known outside of Ireland).

The history of Bulmers dates back to 1935, when it was founded by William Magner in Clonmel, Tipperary. Initially known as Magners, the brand's name changed to Bulmers due to trademark issues in the UK, where there was already a brand with a similar name.

It has always been the market leader in cider in Ireland. Until recently it was probably the *only* cider you'd see in Irish pubs. Bafflingly, it's nearly always on offer in three ways: as a longneck bottle, a draught pint or a pint bottle. The pint bottle has a loyal following when a bit of sun shines and beer gardens all over the country fill with the cacophony of clinking pint glasses filled with ice topped off with bright-orange Bulmers cider – it's a quintessential Irish summer staple.

Bulmers has done a fine job of owning the marketplace but it's not solely their fault craft cider struggles to break through. For a long time, mass-produced ciders tarnished craft ciders' reputation as the cheap flagons are often the drink of choice for underage drinkers and/or anyone looking for a quick fix with a high ABV. It doesn't help that emerging commercial brands 'borrow' from craft cider attributes to convince consumers they are somehow more artisan than they really are (see also 'Craft beer').

PINTS OF OUR PAST

We will always fondly remember (or laugh about) some of the beers that have poured in Irish pubs.

Bass An old-school pale ale, once a favourite of Taoiseach Bertie Ahern.

Caffrey's Best described as a cross between a stout and a lager, popular in the 1990s.

Fürstenberg A German pilsner. Anyone who drank lager in the 1980s seems to be strangely nostalgic about it.

Guinness Light Dubbed 'the *HMS Titanic*' of stouts, it was launched with much fanfare in 1979 but pulled from the market in 1981.

Island's Edge Heineken's ill-fated stout was launched in 2021 and retired in 2023.

Kilkenny Often described as a cross between Guinness and Smithwick's, this one seems to be popping up again recently.

Miller Back when we loved all things American, Miller Draught was a popular choice.

Tennent's A Scottish lager best known for being a cheap option.

BEYOND BEER

Pint glasses are versatile vessels – there are many other drinks we love to sip from them.

Fat Frog

Named after the bright green HB ice pop it tastes like, this is what you get when you mix a bottle of Smirnoff Ice and a bottle of Blue WKD together into a pint glass. Approach with caution.

Pint of blackcurrant

A pint glass filled with a slosh of blackcurrant cordial, lots of ice and topped up with water. There is a distinctive clink of ice in a pint of blackcurrant. It has traditionally had two roles: first, as a hangover cure when you're back in the pub the next day and going straight for a pint is just too much. It's a drink that knows how to quench a thirst. Second, it's often the economical choice for the non-drinker, the designated driver, if you cycled to the pub, etc.

Pint of iced water

It can be the precursor to the hair of the dog or it's for that sensible friend who remembers to down a few pints of iced water while they drink. If only we all remembered to do this!

Pint of milk

In *Milk: The Story of Ireland's Culinary Treasure*, John and Sally McKenna refer to milk as our 'Grand Cru', 'a noble drink', 'the currency of Irish culture'. They say the magic liquid 'deserves to be rewarded with a lexicon that rewards its superb quality. Like fine wine, Irish milk is distinctive, complex, revitalising, renewing.'

It's no wonder, then, that we love to drink it. I don't know many other places in the world where people drink a pint of milk with dinner. It may have fallen out of fashion, but growing up in the 1980s and 1990s, we drank little cartons of milk in school and milk was what we drank at mealtimes. When I first started going to the pub it was the done thing to drink a pint of milk before you went out 'to line the stomach'. The next day, when you were tucking into your homemade roast or pub carvery, a pint of milk was a great settler to go with it.

Rock shandy
The crème de la crème of soft drinks (or minerals or whatever you call them depending on what part of Ireland you're from), a rock shandy is a fine drink – and a distinctly Irish one. Not to be confused with an actual shandy (half lager, half lemonade), it's traditionally made by combining a bottle of Club Orange and a bottle of Club Lemon in a pint glass over ice. It is stunningly refreshing, a hangover favourite and a popular non-alcoholic alternative.

The origin of the pairing is credited to Frank Murphy according to a poster hanging in Jack O'Rourke's pub in Blackrock, Dublin, that says:

> A former Managing Director of C&C, Mr Frank Murphy, was a member of the Blackrock Swimming Club that used to go swimming in the open sea baths in Blackrock. After training on a Sunday morning they would go to O'Rourke's pub in Blackrock for a drink. Their favourite drink was a combination (shandy) of Club Orange and Club Lemon from whence came the name, Rock Shandy.

Shandy
Half lager, half lemonade. Simple and refreshing.

Turbo shandy
Pour a bottle of Smirnoff Ice into a pint glass and top with lager. It's not as bad as it sounds.

CANS VS. PINTS

Technically there shouldn't be any difference. A drink is a drink, right? Yet most of us would say there's no competition. Pints always trump cans. But what about when pints aren't an option? How do we best consume our cans to match the pint drinking – if that's even possible?

If you're drinking cans outside the home, you're most likely drinking straight from the can. That's a different kettle of fish (more on that below). But if you're drinking cans at home or at a house party and are trying to replicate a pint, you're going to want to pour them. That involves a bit more work.

The first hurdle is the glass size. Cans of beer are typically 500ml, whereas your pint glass holds 568ml. Do you just pour it and leave it short? Or do you open another can to top it up and then risk that can getting flat? It's a conundrum. However, there are some easy workarounds.

If you're a Guinness drinker, you'll know they do 538ml cans, which fit perfectly into a regular pint glass. So that solves that problem. It's also easy enough to get hold of 500ml 'pint' glasses for drinking at home. Or if you can find an American pint glass, they hold 16 US fl oz, or 473ml, so that's a bit easier to work with. If you're going to someone else's house, don't assume there's going to be a suitable pint glass. BYOG (bring your own glass) is entirely acceptable, if not encouraged.

Cans have come a long way over the last few years, thanks in part to the pint hiatus during the covid lockdowns (see also 'Takeaway pints'), which meant we all got a bit more inventive about drinking at home. Does anyone remember trying to get hold of jewellery cleaners to recreate the Guinness surge? Some genius discovered that if you took a can of Guinness, pierced a hole in it and allowed the air to escape very slowly, then poured the can into a glass and put the glass in an ultrasonic cleaning unit, the agitation caused the drink to (sort of) surge and partially recreate pouring a draught Guinness. I tried it myself a few times. It was fun but I don't know if it made a difference to the taste.

Guinness never miss a trick. As soon as they realised what we were all at, they got their own brilliant new invention, the Nitro Surge, out into the world. This nifty gadget allows you to pour pub-style pints at home – if you have the gadget, the right cans and the right glass, of course. It's transformed the at-home drinking lives of Guinness drinkers.

Bag of cans

One way cans do come close to pints is in their iconic-ness. Cans – or rather, a bag of cans – feels distinctly Irish and has become a cultural phenomenon in its own right. A bag of cans is so much more than, well, a bag of cans. A bag of cans has a similar meaning to going for a pint. It's non-specific and so specific at the same time. A bag of cans with the lads is even more nuanced (note that 'lads' in Ireland isn't always gender specific).

According to slang.ie, a 'bag of cans' is an Irish party favourite made up of a 'plastic bag containing warm cans of Bulmers', while Urban Dictionary tells us 'a bag of cans with the lads' is 'an Irish phrase used to describe a gathering of lads with plastic bags full of warm beer/cider (usually Dutch Gold or Bulmers) with intent to intake the said alcohol, most likely in an empty field or bush. Has been also known to occur in yer wan's gaff.'

It's all of these things. And more.

REASONS TO DRINK CHEAP CANS

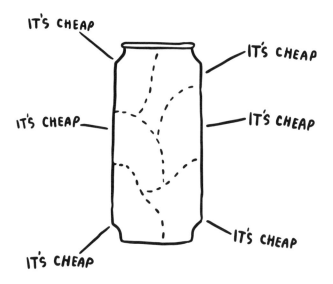

A bag of cans has humble beginnings. At its most basic, it's cheap cans, four to six of them, in a bag. That's it. It's how most of us started out drinking. Before we could go to the pub, it was a bag of cans down the canal/park/river/field/wherever you thought no one would see you, also sometimes known as the Outside Inn. We'd drink them anywhere.

Dutch Gold were the cans in my early bags, a drink choice based purely on the fact that you could get six for £5 (yes, I was drinking long before the euro). Dutch Gold even gets a mention in *Normal People* – does that cement it as iconic? But any cheap lager or cider is acceptable for your classic bag of cans.

Over the last few years, the bag of cans has become its own entity. It's a part of our vocabulary. The covid years played a part in that. All of a sudden, our teenage drinking habits were an acceptable form of socialising again – the pure giddiness of getting out of the house and sitting 2 metres away from someone and having a drink. Few cans? Be grand.

Much like all our beer drinking, the classic bag of cans has evolved. There are new versions now. The plastic bag has made way for the more modern tote bag. A quick online search for 'bag of cans' brings up numerous options for cute, colourful totes you can sling over your arm and fill with cans. And it's not just your bog-standard beers anymore either. Craft beers are getting a good look in. The bag of cans has had a glow-up – and it looks good on it!

CELEBRITY PINTS

Famous people, they're just like us! When they're in Ireland, they love nothing more than sampling a local pint – although often with a photographer or film crew at the ready.

American presidents love to court the Irish-American vote by visiting the old country and, of course, having a pint along the way.

❝ The first time I had Guinness is when I came to the Shannon airport. We were flying into Afghanistan and so stopped in Shannon. It was the middle of the night. And I tried one of these and I realised it tastes so much better here than it does in the States ... You're keeping all the best stuff here! **Barack Obama**

Smithwick's was the pint of choice for Ronald Reagan when he visited O'Farrell's pub in Ballyporeen, Tipperary. His wife Nancy had a glass of locally made Carolans Irish Cream Liqueur.

Bill Clinton went for a pint in 1998 when he was US president with Ireland's then taoiseach, Bertie Ahern. They drank in Bertie's local, Fagan's pub in Drumcondra, Dublin. The *Irish Echo* reported that at 4:30 p.m., Clinton was asked if it was a bit early for a drink. He replied, 'It's never too early for a pint.' He also visited Cassidy's pub on Camden Street for a few scoops.

In 2010, Clinton visited Ireland once again. Journalist Niamh Horan reported being at the Unicorn restaurant when 'a pint of Guinness and a bag of cheese and onion arrived at the next table' – an unusual order at this glitzy spot. It turns out the next table was a motley crew of who's who, including Bill Clinton, Gerry Adams and Denis O'Brien. The pint of Guinness and the crisps 'were ordered by none other than Bono. The U2 rocker phoned ahead and requested that the snack be put in place prior to Mr Clinton's arrival as part of a running joke between the pair.'

JFK visited an excellent pub on an early visit to Dublin before he was president. He's said to have had a drink at Mulligan's pub on Poolbeg Street (disappointingly, it was not a pint he had but a bottle of lager).

Barack Obama caused quite the fanfare when he visited his ancestral home of Moneygall in Offaly. At Ollie Hayes's pub, he poured his own pint, toasted his cousins and sunk it like a pro.

POTUS aren't the only pint drinkers. Celebrities, actors and musicians are all at it.

Game of Thrones star Jason Momoa loves visiting Ireland and a pint of Guinness is his tipple of choice. He likes to share pictures on Instagram from Irish pubs, drinking pints and having the craic.

George Wendt, aka Norm from Cheers, enjoyed a pint in Dingle once. How do I know? Because local restaurant Lord Baker's has a framed picture of him smiling with a lovely-looking pint of Guinness with the caption, 'Cheers, Norm.' Interestingly, he also once starred in a Smithwick's ad, playing himself mingling with the locals at the Gravediggers (John Kavanagh's) pub in Glasnevin on Dublin's northside.

When Beyoncé played at Dublin's Croke Park in 2016, she was photographed swapping her 'lemonade' for a pint of the black stuff backstage. Sláinte, Bey!

Tom Cruise was pictured at the Guinness Storehouse pouring his own pint and looking delighted with himself.

While filming *Star Wars* in Ireland, Mark Hamill (Luke Skywalker!) got behind the bar at the Moorings Bar in Portmagee, Kerry, and poured his own pint, much to the excitement of the locals.

When the Boss himself pops into your pub for a drink, what do you do? Ask him to pull a pint, of course. That's what pub owner Ruth Conlan did when Bruce Springsteen showed up in her Kildare pub, the Burrow. He didn't nail the pint pouring, but he definitely left an impression. Papers reported that Ruth was 'shaking from the exciting and unexpected experience'. The Boss has also been spotted enjoying a pint or two in the Long Hall Pub on South Great George's Street.

When Cruz Beckham turned 18 in 2023, guess where he went for his birthday? Dublin, and pints were high on the agenda. David Beckham shared the celebration on his Instagram, saying, 'God I've missed Dublin' and 'Can't beat a good Irish pub and the people'. There were plenty of pints of the black stuff featured and a visit to the Guinness Storehouse, of course.

Australian actor Hugh Jackman had a great visit to Ireland in 2023, sharing wholesome content of walks and the countryside – and naturally, he took some time out to sample the pub culture. He visited the Guinness Storehouse and was spotted 'splitting the G' in the Duke. He even posted a clip of himself on Instagram getting stuck into a pint of Guinness, proclaiming, 'It's so good.'

The English royals aren't immune to it either. Always hoping to curry favour with the Irish, pints are on the cards when they visit.

When Will and Kate, the Duke and Duchess of Cambridge, came to Ireland, they did the obligatory Guinness Storehouse visit and enjoyed a couple of pints. They've also been spotted sipping pints of plain in London on St Patrick's Day. King Charles has been photographed with a pint in hand on plenty of occasions, but it's his late mother who caused the biggest stir with her pint moment. When Queen Elizabeth visited Ireland in 2011 she also visited the Guinness Storehouse, where she and Prince Philip were given a masterclass in pouring a pint. She was presented with a perfectly poured specimen to try but she didn't even touch it, never mind drink it. As reported in the *Irish Times*, 'Queen Elizabeth gazed at it in fascination. Prince Philip asked whether it was made with Liffey water.' It's hard to tell if Ireland cared that she didn't drink the pint, but it didn't go unnoticed by the rest of the world. That same week, millions of viewers watched Jay Leno parody the moment on the *Tonight Show* when he did a skit that portrayed the Queen as a legless drunk at the Guinness Storehouse.

. . . .

Irish diaspora celebrities always do the best PR when it comes to spreading the word about Irish pints, pubs and the *craic*. Irish celebrity chef Clodagh McKenna, originally from Cork, now lives in the English countryside. She missed her pub fix so much that she's built her own: the Cork Arms is Clodagh's gorgeous homage to an Irish pub. She's even got a Guinness tap. Added bonus? The pub is next door to her 300-year-old home, Broadspear House, which happens to be on the grounds of Highclere Park, best known as the location of *Downton Abbey*. A jolly good pint, I'd say!

. . . .

CHATS AND PINTS

A pint, going for a pint, having a pint – it's not the same as going for drinks and certainly not as ambiguous as going for cocktails. Whether your pint is sipped, savoured or slurped down, it should be straightforward.

You've already established that you will be going to a particular type of place (that serves pints) and what you will probably be drinking (pints). There most likely won't be a menu to peruse, discuss, dissect or make decisions about. Pints are just pints. You order them and you sip them and you get down to the real reason you go for a pint: the chats, the banter, the slagging, the laughing, the confiding.

When a pint means a chat, as it so often does, it can be the best kind of chat. Maybe it's the fact that the alcohol loosens you up a bit, but it's also the simplicity, the straightforwardness of the pint that invites a good chat. And these days, when so much of our chat is virtual – texts, WhatsApps, DMs, etc. – it makes those IRL (in real life) chats all the more precious, don't you think? A pint is just an added bonus.

Catch-ups
Should be a nice, easy-going affair. Not too deep, bitta *craic*, feels wholesome. Whether it's a catch-up with a pal, a pint to dissect a day at work with a colleague (see also 'After-work pints'), a catch-up over Christmas (see also 'Christmas pints') or with your cousin at a funeral (see also 'Funeral pints'), there is a sweet spot of conversation that comes with having a pint (or a few).

Banter

This usually happens with a group of pals. It can involve slagging, but light-hearted slagging only. Belly laughs are an added bonus.

The word 'banter' has been usurped of late as a flirting term (thanks, *Love Island*) but I'm talking about old-school banter. Proper chats. How to differentiate? I turned to Irish journalist Jim Carroll for help on that. Jim has been running a series of talks called Banter since 2009, where they 'tell stories about this, that and the other'.

" When we started our series of talks, interviews and conversations back in 2009, Banter was the name we picked because it made total sense to us and summed up what we wanted the series to be. Remember, this was pre banter becoming 'banter', a term which has to come with inverted commas these days.

To us, banter was an old-fashioned term which meant a load of people coming together in big rooms or small rooms and having a whale of a time. It's a term which served us well over the years. It was the perfect encapsulation of what we set out to do: have a bunch of folks talking about all manner of ideas and topics and themes in an informal, laid-back and casual way. It was not about the dreaded chats or debates or any of that malarkey, but something which was both light and heavy – and happy to stay talking all night if the mood was right.

Which is exactly the kind of banter that can come with a few pints.

The D&Ms (deep and meaningfuls)
These can be joyous or they can be treacherous. The deep and meaningfuls usually happen after a few pints. Sometimes you really need them. Maybe there's something you want to get off your chest. Perhaps there's a break-up that needs dissecting. Maybe there's a crush you need to confess. Or a night that went awry that you'd like to unload. For the most part this is healthy enough but it all depends on who you have the D&Ms with.

The heated debate
This is the one to avoid. There are good reasons why 'no religion, no politics' is accepted as a general rule in all pubs.

THE CHIPPER AND PINTS

Have you even had a proper night on the pints if you don't end up in the chipper? Pints and the chipper afterwards go together like salt and vinegar.

The Irish chipper is a particular thing – and an essential part of our pint culture. Even just writing the word *chipper*, I can almost smell it. I can certainly picture it clearly. The glow of the chipper on the street when you leave the pub is like a lighthouse guiding you home. Pub, chipper, taxi, bed.

The chipper is always a good idea.

The Irish chipper has been supporting pint drinkers for quite some time. They were originally set up by Italian families who arrived in Ireland in the 1880s from a small set of villages in Valle di Comino in southern Italy. Before they brought the idea of the chipper over from the UK, Italians would sell ice cream in the summer and roast chestnuts in the winter. But once they started frying, we were hooked. As more Italians came to

There is an annual festival celebrating Ireland in Italy and it's not St Patrick's Day. Every August, the Italian village of Casalattico holds Irish Fest, a celebration of the Irish-Italian connection and the local families that moved to Ireland, many of whom set up chippers. There's Irish music, beers, dancing and of course fish 'n' chips.

BIG
BAG
OF
~~CANS~~
CHIPS

Ireland over the years, more chippers appeared. These days, the Italian-Irish chipper culture is part of the fabric of the country. Almost every town has one.

Chipper cuisine complements pints perfectly. A steamy bag of something fried is going to benefit you come the morning. Their menus tend to be extensive – there is something for everyone – but there are a few specific things that suit post-pints particularly well.

Bag of chips
The gold standard. Chips should be piping hot, fresh out of the fat, and doused in salt and vinegar. Then they go straight into the bag. And this is the key difference between a proper chipper and anywhere else you get chips: they fill the first bag, the smaller one, to the brim with chips and fold that closed, then that goes into another, slightly bigger bag and the unspoken rule is that a few extra chips go in there too. Genius! This means you can pick out a few straightaway for the walk home and the rest stay toasty until you can tuck in.

Battered sausage
A popular post-pub snack and a great addition to the bag of chips. Chips and battered sausage, please. Extra vinegar.

Curry chips/garlic chips/cheesy garlic chips/super chips

Modern places will serve these and call them loaded fries and charge you double or more what the chipper does but the chipper is the OG of covering your chips with gloop. Chips in a foil tray with sauce all over it? We love it. The curry sauce really comes alive in the later hours with a rake of pints beforehand. The garlic and cheesy chips are for eating alone. The lesser-seen super chips are covered in gravy.

Snack box

Two pieces of golden fried chicken and chips served in a cardboard box. Although this is very, very tasty, it's messy – approach eating in company with caution. A tub of gravy on the side should be considered if available.

Spice burger

An Irish chipper stalwart, these mysterious burgers are made from a secret recipe of beef, onions, breadcrumbs, herbs and spices. They almost disappeared from our menus in 2009, but lucky for us, they were saved.

Wurly burger

The lesser-spotted wurly burger is worth seeking out. A wurly burger is when you swap out your regular burger or quarter pounder for a battered burger. This is soakage at its best.

....

Pop megastar Rihanna filmed some of her iconic 'We Found Love' music video in a chipper called Brennan's in Co. Down. In the video, she can be seen dancing on the table in front of the menu boards. We've all been there, Riri.

....

CHRISTMAS PINTS

Christmas pints are a lot, and in more ways than one. December is when we actualise the pints we talked about all year, stacking catch-ups into our calendars. There are work pints, friends pints, cousin pints, family pints, old school friend pints, pints when you arrive home, pints because you are home, shopping pints, popping into town pints, someone's birthday pints (isn't there always a birthday at Christmas?), Christmas Eve pints, Stephen's Day pints, the in-between-days pints, New Year's Eve pints, New Year's Day pints and pints before you leave again pints.

Work Christmas pints
Whether it's the official work do or just a night in the pub with the work gang, these are likely the earliest pints in the calendar. It marks the start of Christmas proper. There's usually a good build-up to it, mostly because it's preferable to talk about where you're going, what you're wearing or who's going to get the drunkest instead of talking about actual work at work.

A few things might happen. Someone will get very drunk, very early. Someone sensible will do the Irish goodbye (see also page 105) you wish you had done. There will be secrets shared, tales told and maybe even some hook-ups. Depending on where you work, drinking with your work friends will either be great or it will be a disaster. But still, there is something satisfying about getting work to pay for your drinks and getting loose-lipped (chats or otherwise) with people you normally talk shop with. It's fun. Most of the time. As long as you're not the one everyone is talking about the next day.

Christmas shopping pint(s)

You head to the shops for the last few presents or wrapping paper; any excuse will do. You've already sent out that text to see who's around and plan to meet a friend for a quick pint somewhere cosy and Christmassy before you head home. It's unseasonably warm and probably drizzling with rain. You arrive. The pub is packed, you're sweating and your shopping bags are in the way but you find a nook with a few free seats. You remove all your layers and stow the shopping under a sticky table. You send out the text: 'Got a seat!' So you may as well stay for another one. A few others arrive. The pints are flowing. Crisps are eaten. The last bus beckons but you're having belly laughs with people you might not see again until next year. These are some of the best pints, despite the bag of shopping you left under the table.

Homecoming pints/Christmas Eve pints

If you've lived away from home, particularly abroad, you know all about the homecoming pints or Christmas Eve pints and you either love them or loathe them. You'll love them if you have the ideal scenario of a local to return to where they know you and what you drink and you bump into all the people you want to see. Bliss.

Or you'll loathe the more likely scenario, which involves returning to a pub you'd no longer drink in by choice. You don't know anyone there except for people you don't want to see. It takes ages to get served, everyone's too young and you know if you don't leave early enough, you won't get a bus or taxi and will have to ring home to get collected and you'll never hear the end of it. But then they play 'Fairytale of New York' and you throw your arms around whoever is beside you and sing along and get teary-eyed. Despite the debacle of getting a lift home or the hangover when you're peeling the spuds the next day, you know you'll do the exact same thing next year.

The 12 pubs of Christmas

It may be out of fashion or even fully cancelled these days, but for a brief moment in time, the 12 pubs of Christmas was brilliant – iconic, even. It reflected all that we love about Christmas pints: camaraderie, *craic*, Christmas jumpers and catching up with friends.

The basic rules were simple: visit 12 different pubs and have a drink in each pub. But 12 pints! Even the most hollowed-legged would struggle with 12 pints. If that didn't seem like a mammoth enough task, people took it upon themselves to complicate things and come up with additional rules. These rules were usually created by that friend who has too much time on their hands and thinks they are hilarious – a dangerous combination. Some of the silly rules weren't too bad, like put your jumper on backwards or swap your drink orders around. If you slipped up there was usually a penalty, which could be to skull your drink or drink a penalty shot. So far, so much potential to get messy. But the more drinks you had, the harder these simple tasks became. No swearing! Drinking only with the wrong hand! Before you knew it, you were dancing with a stranger or smoking for the first time in years and you'd probably gained a Santa hat. Having done the 12 pubs only once in my life, I can understand why so many pubs have banned them. RIP the 12 pubs of Christmas.

CRAFT BEER

Our attitude to craft beer in Ireland hasn't always been favourable. When something new and different comes along, our instant reaction is often to slag it off, like calling it a hipster fad or dismissing craft beer as cat piss, sentiments bandied around by beer drinkers all over Ireland. Admittedly I've never drunk cat piss but I have a feeling commercial beers might come closer in taste than the excellent craft beers being brewed in Ireland.

It's baffling because in so many other parts of life, we want variety and options. We want to support local and Irish. But our pubs are still predominantly Big Beer. Yes, I'm aware this book is pretty much dedicated to Big Beer but that's because when it came to writing about the modern culture of Irish pints, for the most part that still means — and has always meant — mass-produced commercial drinks. We order the same stouts, lagers and sugary ciders. It's what we know and it's what we're comfortable with (see also 'Brand loyalty').

It's not all bad news for craft beer. The market share is growing, slowly, but it's going in the right direction. By mid-2023 there were 79 independent production microbreweries in the Republic of Ireland and craft beer production had increased by 30% from 2017 to 2022. Cans of craft are in every shop. It's only a matter of time before we see more taps appear (fingers crossed).

Here's hoping this 'hipster fad' continues to tap away at Big Beer despite the odds being stacked against it.

CRAIC AGUS CEOL:
MUSIC AND PINTS

There are few things that feel as Irish as having a pint in a cosy pub with a crackling fire while you tap your foot to a bit of traditional music, or trad, as it's better known. We call it *craic agus ceol* (fun and music). We love it. Tourists love it. It's exported all around the world (see also 'The Irish pub'). At their very core, trad pubs, singing pubs, *ceol* pubs and session pubs are of one of the most Irish things we have and a pint goes perfectly with every note.

Music has long been an important part of Irish culture, a way of carrying stories and bringing people together. The trad session evolved from the Irish custom of people gathering in homes, and later, pubs, for a night of music, storytelling, dancing and a few drinks. There could be singers, fiddles, guitars, tin whistles, accordions, uilleann pipes, bodhráns or any combination of these. Informal, organic gatherings like this have always been at the heart of Irish culture and the session in a pub these days is a direct descendant of that.

It had a few bumps along the way, though, writes Kevin Martin in his book *Have Ye No Homes to Go To*: 'Before the 1950s, it had become uncommon to hear music in bars in Ireland.' He implies the joy had been sucked out of things by the 'virtually theocratic state', or the fun police as we'd call them these days. He laments that traditional music and dancing had receded from public places to the homes and cottages of Ireland.

But as the Irish emigrated, Martin writes, they brought the music with them: 'Irish traditional music sessions in pubs were popular overseas before they took off in Ireland.' He mentions that the Session website (thesession.org) claims that the first Irish music session that took place in a pub was the Devonshire Arms in Kentish Town, London in 1948. Sessions were happening all around the US and the UK and worked their way back to Ireland. Folk music also played a role, becoming hugely popular in the 1960s: 'The Clancy Brothers, the Chieftains, the Dubliners, the Dublin City Ramblers, the Wolfe Tones and later Sweeney's Men and Planxty were some of the more successful bands.'

Irish pubs began to reconfigure themselves to suit the new bands and in turn music sessions and a renewed love for trad music. Some pubs might let it be known that they would sponsor a session on a certain afternoon or evening – sponsor meaning the musicians would get a few free pints in return for playing. It became commonplace in villages, towns and cities all over Ireland.

Trad sessions have become more organised now and are a huge draw for tourists but the really special moments of pints and music in Irish pubs are the impromptu ones when you're in a pub and someone breaks out in *sean-nós* singing (old style). The whole pub hushes and listens. If you're *really* listening, you might close your eyes and nod or sway along. You're carried away in the moment and the melody. The singing is met with rapturous applause, knee slaps and plenty of *yewww*s and *hup*s. There's nothing like it.

But despite how good you think you are, think twice before you grab a tin whistle or volunteer yourself to sing. Is it a singing pub? There are many pubs where no matter who you are, there's still no singing. Liam Clancy is rumoured to have been told to stop singing in Mulligan's of Poolbeg Street and Kathleen Behan is said to have been one of the only people allowed to sing in Grogan's.

AND IT'S
NO NAY
NEVER

NO NAY
NEVER
NO MORE!

If singing is allowed, is yours the right kind of song? Laments or rebellion songs may be preferred. Again, it depends on the pub. An upbeat song like 'The Rattlin' Bog' could be sung the odd time but read the room and know your audience. There's a fine line between entertaining and draining when it comes to singing in pubs.

If you do want to prepare, learn a few songs from the Dubliners – many are belted out at singalongs over a few scoops, including 'The Irish Rover', 'The Wild Rover', 'Dirty Old Town', 'Fields of Athenry' and 'Whiskey in the Jar'. Add to that anything by Christy Moore, Mary Black or the Chieftains and you're all set.

Legendary DJ Annie Macmanus gets it. Here she is writing about 'My Lagan Love', a Chieftain's song, in a 2020 *Irish Times* article about being homesick for Ireland:

❝ When you hear a song like 'Lagan Love', a song so dripping in Irish mysticism, you think of rolling landscapes and stone walls and low-roofed pubs with snugs and auld fellas at the bar who stand up and sing folk songs after a rake of pints. You think of circles of session musicians, feet stamping on the floor, bursts of laughter and glasses clinking. Of every Guinness advert that ever existed.

CRISPS AND PINTS

There are many excellent foods that pair well with pints and with beers in general, but what is the one food that is nearly always in close proximity to a pint? Crisps. Is a pub without a few packets of crisps really even a pub? How many times has a packet of crisps kept you going till dinner or maybe even was your dinner?

Crisps are to Ireland what tapas are to Spain. Hear me out! In Spain, tapas are defined as small, savoury snacks served with drinks. Eh, sounds like crisps in Ireland? Tick. The Spanish are masters of all things tapas. The Irish? Masters of crisps. Tick. In Spain, there are myriad unwritten rules around how you eat and serve tapas. It's the same eating crisps in Ireland. Tick. Tapas are great fun to eat. Crisps? Great *craic*! Tick.

Allow me to elaborate. The Irish love crisps. We eat them as snacks, in sandwiches, on the side of sandwiches, as a stopgap for dinner, at house parties and at kids' parties. And we love to eat them in the pub.

It starts young. If you grew up in Ireland and went to the pub as a child, you'd be expecting a packet of crisps with a fizzy drink, maybe a Cidona or Club Orange, to keep you quiet while the grown-ups sipped a pint. When you move on to pints yourself, the crisp habit sticks around. Crisps and pints go hand in hand – literally. You're out for a few afternoon scoops, someone comes back from the bar and they've added a few bags of crisps to the order. Smiles all round.

TAPAS

The Irish may not have actually invented crisps but we've certainly mastered them. The invention of crisps is usually credited to a chef called George Crum in Saratoga Springs, New York, in the 1950s. Apparently, a customer complained that his potato fries (chips to us) were too thick, so the chef sliced the spuds wafer-thin, fried them and doused them in salt. The American potato chip (crisps to us) was born.

In the UK, a grocer named Frank Smith started making crisps around 1910 and started selling them to pubs in Cricklewood, so no doubt there were a few Irish tucking into his packets of unseasoned crisps that came with a small blue sachet of salt to sprinkle over them.

It was in Dublin, though, that the crisps we know and love today came to be. Tatyo founder Joe 'Spud' Murphy is widely credited for creating the first-ever cheese and onion flavoured crisps in 1954.

Mr Tayto, North and South

A beloved character that's been on the packets of Tayto crisps ever since they were invented, Mr Tayto is practically a national mascot. In 2007 he ran in the general election

Southern Tayto are sometimes called 'Free Staytos'.

and in 2009 he released his autobiography, *The Man Inside the Jacket*. Ireland even briefly had a theme park dedicated to Mr Tayto and all things crisps, Tayto Park (now rebranded as Emerald Park).

And then there is his rival/cousin of sorts, Mr Tayto Northern Ireland. Northern Ireland Tayto was set up in Tandragee, Co. Armagh by Thomas Hutchinson, who in 1956 made a deal with Joe 'Spud' Murphy to use the name Tayto for his new crisps as long as they weren't sold in the Republic of Ireland. These Northern Irish Tayto have their own Mr Tayto, who's just as jolly.

Proper pub crisps

Pub crisps are a different breed. They should not be the multipack corn snacks you'll find at kids' birthday parties. They should not be in garish bags with wacky flavours of the ilk you see jostling for attention in forecourt shops. For proper pub crisps, we're talking about classic flavours, and really, there are only a handful of acceptable brands.

The crisp selection in a pub could be an indicator of exactly what sort of a pint situation you're getting into. Seeing only Pringles behind the bar doesn't fill me with confidence. And while the new wave of Irish crisps like Keogh's, O'Donnells and Clintons are all excellent crisps and go perfectly well with a pint, they simply haven't proven themselves as a lifelong partner to the pint yet.

When it comes to crisps and pints, I still need the added seasoning of nostalgia. The traditional crisp brands I want to see in a pub are Tayto, King or Manhattan. As for the flavours? Cheese and onion or salt and vinegar will do nicely. And while they aren't technically crisps, Smiths Bacon Fries and Smiths Scampi Fries are pub stalwarts and excellent choices to add an air of sophistication to your 'tapas'. A few bags of Manhattan Nuts are also a delicious and nutritious pint snack.

....

In proper pub crisp etiquette, it's polite to open the bag right side up, then tear along the seam on the side, allowing the packet to open flat for easy sharing.

....

THE DIASPORA AND PINTS

Surely no one has done more for the reputation of Ireland, and in turn our pubs and pints, than the Irish diaspora. For generations we've emigrated all over the world, carrying with us nostalgic, romantic notions of the country left behind – and the pubs, of course.

When we leave the country we all seem to become spokespeople for how amazing Ireland is, whereas at home we love to give out. About the weather, the economy, politics, RTÉ, the HSE, the clampers, Ryanair, overpriced pints (see also 'Price of pints'), overpriced ice cream, TV shows, buses, trains, the cold, potholes, badly made tea, the price of butter, the snow, the heat. And so on.

At home we are begrudgers. We don't like people who are too positive or anyone who has notions. It's almost part of our heritage to begrudge anyone doing well. We love to say, 'I told you so.'

But when we leave the country? It's all 'Cut me and I bleed green!' We will happily wrap ourselves in the tricolour and wax lyrical about being the island of saints and scholars. We turn up the U2 and pepper our chat with *cúpla focal* (in Irish, 'a few words') just to let everyone know we have our very own language.

And as for the pint? We seek them out, the proper kind, an Irish pint that we imagine will somehow transport us back to the country we've forgotten we used to give out about so much. It's no wonder there are not only Irish but also Irish pubs all around the globe (see also 'The Irish pub').

DISTANCE FROM IRELAND

LOVE FOR IRELAND

Pints as currency

To really understand how much currency the Irish pint has globally, let me tell you about John McDonagh, a long-time New York cab driver and the son of immigrants from Co. Donegal. In 2022, McDonagh flew from New York to Dublin to claim a two-pint IOU taxi fare.

The cabbie had picked up Dubliner Shane Gaffney in New York in 2013. When Gaffney didn't have enough money to cover the fare, he instead offered McDonagh an IOU for two pints of Guinness in Dublin.

'I got the IOU nine years ago. I get in the cab, it's four in the morning. He didn't have the full fare and he said he owns a bar in Dublin,' John told the *Irish Independent*. 'Then he wrote out on a trip sheet that when I come to Dublin, I can go to Gaffney and Son to get two pints of Guinness. We discussed how much a pint was and the exchange rate between the dollar and the euro. We were like Wall Street brokers. This was unique that someone said they'd pay me in Guinness,' he added.

It turns out Gaffney's family business is a pub in Fairview, Dublin. He was delighted to finally pay his debt to McDonagh and did so with plenty of fanfare and a few column inches.

EARLY HOUSES

Early houses are pubs that have been granted a licence that means they can open at 7 a.m., the idea being they could cater to workers who might want a drink at unsociable hours because of their jobs, like market or dock workers, fishermen, bakers, etc. In Dublin, you'd usually find them on Capel Street or near the docks.

As times changed, the early houses became popular for another reason. Instead of hard workers, hard partygoers began to seek them out as Dublin's nightlife became busier in the late 1990s and early 2000s.

There's an RTÉ Radio documentary called *Early House* recorded in 1999 in the Cobblestone, one of the early houses at that time. A local is interviewed and he recalls the pub and who drank there:

" But I do remember well, of the shop, and who drank in the shop, and of the local women, used to come into the snug and out around the shop itself. There's an awful lot of dealers used to drink in here. Cattle dealers, horse dealers, etc. You still get that feeling of the past and they'd always give you the nod of the head to welcome you, with a smile. And that is a great thing to come into any public house and get. You won't get that in any other place in Dublin.

As time went on, the clientele became more varied. Depending on where you were, you were likely to rub shoulders with wired shift workers (postmen, nurses, etc.), thirsty early risers, tourists who had landed in Dublin early and all-night revellers who had no intention of going to bed yet.

The 7 a.m. starts are less common these days, with only a handful in Dublin that will still have the shutters up and the doors open for a breakfast pint. Speaking of breakfast, one place that will probably continue to open early is Slattery's on Capel Street thanks to Anthony Bourdain. Bourdain visited the pub on a trip to Dublin and featured the Slattery's full Irish and a pint of Guinness on his TV show, making it a go-to for Bourdain fans visiting the city.

They may be a dying breed these days but thanks to the brilliant website brandnewretro.ie, which is home to a compendium of Irish pop culture magazine scans, we can get a glimpse into what an early house looked like in their 2003 heyday.

EARLY HOUSE ETIQUETTE

There is a hilarious article from *The Slate* magazine, a satirical Dublin-based monthly funny magazine, called 'The Early House of Horrors'. It 'profiled the dodgy spots that serve booze in the morning time'. They also printed a list of early house etiquette to abide to:

1   Don't talk to anyone who has a plastic bag on the table in front of them. This could contain a gun, some heroin, a dead baby, or their soiled underpants – none of which you want to engage with at that stage of a night out.
2   Don't be the first to start dancing. There will almost always be some clueless West Brit who can take on this dangerous role.
3   Ignore anyone who points a needle at you in the jacks.
4   Rolling joints on the bar is not on.
5   Neither is doing lines.
6   Don't ask for cocktails.
7   Dancing around in sunglasses may seem appropriate to your exhausted brain. Everyone else will be saying 'that dickhead thinks he's George Michael'.
8   Don't try to put on a Dublin accent. As is only proper, you will have your head kicked in if you pretend to be a local while talking about the oneness of life and gurning your head off.
9   Ladies especially, don't go to the toilet on the pavement outside the pub – even if you think you are hidden behind a car or your friend. It may seem like a festival atmosphere to you, but for everyone else, it's midday on a Saturday and they are heading into town to go shopping.
10 Don't get involved in a blood feud, even if the guy who has explained it to you seems to be 100% in the right.

ECUMENICAL PINTS

The essential pint moments in life aren't too dissimilar to the sacraments: first pints, wedding pints, funeral pints. So it seems fitting to include a list of ecumenical pints.

I know, I know, most of us will think of the TV show *Father Ted* when we say 'ecumenical'. 'That would be an ecumenical matter, Father!' was a favourite coverall answer the priests in *Father Ted* liked to use and it's become a catchphrase in its own right. But the actual definition of ecumenical is 'of or relating to the Christian Church throughout the world, especially with regard to its unity'.

So when I talk about ecumenical pints, I'm referring to all the opportunities for pints that the Christian Church, in particular the Catholic Church, affords us. There are so many holy days, religious days and holidays that, let's face it, we find a place for a drink – at least in Ireland, anyway. And without getting too philosophical (or should I say ecumenical?) about the whole thing, the Catholic Church based most of their celebrations and sacraments around pagan rituals that already existed, so are they really even ecumenical to begin with?

Wetting the baby's head
Baptism is the initiation into the church, a welcoming ritual where a baby's head is cleansed with water, often while it's wearing an elaborate white dress. Everyone else is dressed in their finery for family photos, with proud godparents making promises.

The baby's head isn't the only thing that gets wet. These days the phrase is more likely to mean having a few pints to celebrate. The baby is probably asleep for most of the day anyway, so the pub is an ideal place to congregate afterwards for a bite to eat and a few drinks.

It's been the done thing for a long time. In Kevin Martin's book *Have Ye No Homes to Go To?: The History of the Irish Pub*, he touches on drinking at baptisms when he talks about a 1944 study, Attitudes Towards Drinking in Ireland, by Robert Bales:

> ❝ Bales distinguished between the symbolic use of alcohol accompanying spiritual activities and the celebratory use of alcohol in social rituals in Irish culture. He gave the example of baptism. The drinking 'was convivial, not part of the ritual ... though it had a social meaning. He who offered liberally was regarded as "a good fellow" and his offering implied that he regarded the other as "a good fellow". The exchange was symbolic of social solidarity and acceptability on both sides, without explicit religious meaning.'

Who wouldn't want to be considered a good fellow? Better get the pints in, so.

Communions and confirmations

The kids are more involved in these sacraments and so are more likely to have an influence on the celebrations. You may end up at a party fuelled by sweets or a day at an amusement park but if you're lucky the celebrations will happen in a hotel, pub or restaurant. And if so, you can guarantee there will be a congregation at the bar for a pint.

Special shoutout for the confirmation that unwittingly sets the foundations for seeking out a pint from a young age by convincing teenagers to pledge that they won't drink until they're 18. Confirmation age, then, is when many of us start counting down the days until we can drink and thus start to consider drinking to be a reward.

The confirmation 'pledge' is a hangover from the Irish Temperance movement in the 1800s – it's claimed that 3–4 million people in Ireland took the pledge between 1839 and 1845.

And it's not just about the pints we enjoy at religious celebrations. In his book *Dublin Pub Life and Lore*, social historian Kevin C. Kearns goes through the many parallels between the Church and the pub in Ireland:

> Each has its authority figure, devout patrons, rituals and spatial patterns. Both offer their own solace to bedraggled souls weary of the outside world. Parallels even exist between priest and publican. Both enjoy exalted status of respect and power and hear confessions, one dispensing advice and the other absolution. And one cannot ignore the religious symbolisms associated with the public house – the barman was long known as the 'curate'; afternoon closing time was the 'holy hour'; snugs were termed 'confession boxes'; a black pint of Guinness with its white collar is called the 'parish priest'; regulars are the 'faithful'; persons barred feel 'excommunicated'; pubs closed to women were the 'holy ground'; privileged bar space was the 'inner sanctum'; and when notorious pubman Brendan Behan would crawl from pub to pub he proclaimed he was 'doing the stations of the cross'.

Holy hour

If you're in the Church, holy hour refers to a devotional tradition of spending an hour in Eucharistic adoration in the presence of the Blessed Sacrament. If you were in or near a pub in Ireland from the 1920s up until 2000, it meant you could be kicked out in the middle of the day.

'Holy hour' came in two varieties. On Sunday, all pubs were required to close between 2 p.m. and 4 p.m. in an attempt to make sure 'the men' went home for their dinner after mass and didn't stay out drinking. For the unruly folk in Dublin and Cork, it happened every day between 2:30 p.m. and 3:30 p.m. to ensure workers would leave the pub after lunch and go back to work.

But in true Irish form, there were ways around it. For the most part, you could stay in the pub if the bar person didn't mind; it just meant the doors were closed. This excerpt I found in *The Pure Drop: A Book of Irish Drinking* by John Killen really sums it up. It's from a short story by Pete St John called 'Jaysus Wept':

❝ Dublin languished in the wintry, pagan afternoon ... It was the Holy Hour, when the city's publicans make the supreme sacrifice by closing their doors to the general public for sixty minutes. The great daily drama of clearing the house had begun. Credentials were checked in that secret, timeless way known only to the selected few. The hardcore. The privileged ones. They would stay behind. All else were banished to the grim city streets. Soon the shutters went into place and the doors were locked. The inner sanctum brotherhood of drinkers reigned incarnate. At least now there would be peace. A Holy house when the true sense of belonging was something one experienced but never spoke about. Your acceptance in the local was in Dublin a saviour. A sanctuary. Beyond explaining. Here men knew their place and did their duty. They knew their station in life. Their value as human beings. So the great limbo of knowing descended. Inchoate. Price-less. Now it was indeed the Holy Hour. Full of nods and winks and whispers. The ticking of the grandfather clock was like a prologue to the drama. To the drink. To thinking. To rehabilitation and freedom... To letting mind run riot in safety.

VERY GD

FRIDAY

Good Friday pints

Good Friday was a perfect example of the over-the-top chokehold that religion has had on Irish public life. The Roman Catholic Church observes Good Friday as a day of fasting and abstinence, so until 2018 pubs and licensed premises (bar a few exceptions) weren't allowed to open on Good Friday. This had been the case since 1927.

For decades, the rebellious and the thirsty went to great lengths to plan parties and piss-ups in kitchens and shebeens around the country. There would be queues in the shops and off-licences the night before. The savvy drinker knew you could still get served in hotels if you were booked in or at some train stations. Some would even go so far as to get on the ferry to Holyhead or France and drink all the way there and back again.

It all changed in 2018. For the first time in over 90 years, we could walk into a bar and legally order a pint on Good Friday. There was plenty of celebration. There were news reports all day, with TV cameras in pubs watching the first pints being poured to happy customers.

These days it's just another Friday but it's also the perfect excuse to go to the pub, don't you think?

EXPERTS ON PINTS

Oscar Wilde once said an expert is 'an ordinary man away from home giving advice'. Isn't that all of us in the pub? Sure we're all experts when we're ordering a pint and it's no wonder. The myth, the lore, the marketing, the romantic notions we're surrounded by when it comes to Irish pubs – and pints in Irish pubs – means it's second nature to us.

The image of how a pint should be poured and how it should look is ingrained in our minds. Particularly stout, and particularly Guinness. Anna Kinsella was spot on when she wrote about this in 'Nine ways of looking at a pint of Guinness' for *Vittles*:

> For many people, even without the word Guinness adorning it, the drink would be instantly recognisable in a way no other alcoholic beverage is.
>
> This image is sticky. Its steadiness helps it to stay in the mind. Sticky images are powerful. They create expectations. If I order a pint of Guinness and what is served doesn't look how I imagine it will, I know that something has gone wrong. But when it is correct, beautiful even, it is reinforcing an unspoken set of guidelines set down by people on barstools across Ireland and beyond, combined with over a century of vivid, distinctive branding and advertising. Together, this process and its results are capable of turning every conscientious Guinness drinker into a guardian of the brand.

The image is sticky – it is! We know what we should expect. We know how we should hold it. And yes, we are all guardians of the brand. We're like human billboards every time we put a pint of Guinness in our hand.

Never mind that once we start talking about the pints, we discuss them in depth. We rate them, debate them. We praise them, we critique them. We talk about pints with the same vigour that critics have for art or food. We brush over the fact that the beverage we are dissecting is one of the most mass produced beers in the world. We are all connoisseurs when it comes to our pints.

Looking to brush up on your 'expertise'? Here's a handy guide to sounding like an expert.

LOVELY SHTICK
GREAT DOMEAGE
SURE THE KEG IS JUST THERE
WOULD YA LOOK AT THE LACING ON THAT?
SURE THAT'S A MECCA FOR PINTS
YOU'D NEARLY STICK A FLAKE IN THAT
BUT WILL IT PASS THE TILT TEST?
NICE AND CREAMY

FESTIVAL PINTS

We love a festival in Ireland – music, arts, jazz, comedy, horses, ploughing, food, matchmaking. You name it, we have a festival for it.

And it's nothing new either. We've had an enduring relationship with festivals, fairs and celebrations going right back to pre-Christian Ireland. Long before we had Electric Picnic and Kilkenny Cat Laughs, our ancestors' calendar year revolved around Imbolc, Bealtaine, Lughnasa, Samhain and the quarter-day festivities that came with them. And I'd wager they involved drink too.

These days, music festivals and outdoor gigs are the markers of the year. When the big names are announced, it makes the news headlines. When the tickets go on sale, we chart our elation or disappointment about getting tickets online. We flock to them in our tens of thousands. We dress up in the merch for concerts. We walk for miles to get to them. You'd better believe we're going to have a pint when we get there.

But the pints – ah, festival pints. Are they the worst pints we have? Possibly. But do we drink them anyway? Definitely! Sure, what choice do we have?

The fact that the bar is usually a trek (or feels like it) is the first hurdle. You're in the zone, you've got your spot and you're waiting for the band to start but it's your round and you have to get to the bar. It's either mucky or too hot. Either way, your wellies are uncomfortable. Maybe it's even raining, in which case your poncho probably has a leak. When you finally get to the bar, you realise everyone else is there too. There's a queue snaking around the crowd control barriers with 80 people ahead of you. You join them. You make some small talk or inhale the joint being smoked beside you. You'd go on your phone but there's no reception.

When you eventually make it to the top, there's a choice of probably two drinks: a lager you'd never normally drink or a sugary cider. You order five pints from the bar staff who seemed like they were in a hurry to take your order but are now moving at a snail's pace. You really hope they'll pour them fresh but you can't bring yourself to ask. Instead, they just take them from the table behind them that's laid out full of lacklustre, flat pints in plastic glasses. The bar staff put four of them in a holder for you, one of those flimsy cardboard things that wraps around the top of the pint and the plastic glasses hang from it. On the walk back you lose at least 30% of the warming, flat beer because they're hopping around in the crappy holder while you try to sip the one in your hand. The beer sloshes on the jeans you were planning on wearing all weekend, or worse, goes down your leg if you've got shorts on and into the socks in your uncomfortable wellies.

You arrive back and the gang is delighted to see you. They help you coax the wobbly plastic glasses out from their holder, spilling another load as they do. But everyone's got a 'pint' now. They're delighted. The band comes on, you sip your dead pint and think, 'This is fucking brilliant.' Until it's time to go to the bar again.

Despite all this, we will continue to go to festivals and drink festival pints. We love it, really.

FESTIVAL BEER

FIRST PINTS

There's often an expected experience of a first pint. A parent or sibling taking you down to the local on your 18th birthday, pulling up a stool at the bar, introducing you to their cronies and asking, 'So what'll you have?' You take a look around, assess the situation and settle on whatever they're all drinking. A cheer, a sip, a smile. A pat on the back. Welcome to adulthood! Sounds perfect, doesn't it? Like a Werther's Original ad but about pints.

But this certainly wasn't the case for me and I doubt it was for you either, especially if you're Irish. There weren't many of us in the 1990s anyway who waited until we were 18 to have that first pint. As mentioned in 'Ecumenical pints', from the moment I made that confirmation pledge I was planning and plotting when I'd have a drink. But it wasn't just about the drink. It was about being an adult. It was about transgressing being a teenager. There were a lot of things that would accomplish that, and getting served in a pub was one of them.

I think I ordered my first pint at the bar when I was 15. I was in Cork visiting my older sister, who was just barely 18 herself. I don't know exactly how it happened but I remember going to the bar and getting served. I think I probably ordered a Budweiser because it was the 1990s and I'd drunk bottles of it before. Although I do remember I was wearing a football jumper that had Carlsberg emblazoned across it, so maybe it was a Carlsberg. The jumper stands out in my mind because I was so impressed with myself that I got served in it.

That first pint probably worked out because I hadn't planned it or thought about it. There were also many more times when we *did* plan it — picked our outfits, a time, a location and built up the suspense — only to be turned away at the door or the bar. And rightly so. There were a few main challenges to getting served when you were underage.

Not getting served because the barman knows you

There was no way I was walking into a pub in my hometown at 15 looking to get served. The plight of anyone from a village or small to mid-sized town in Ireland is that everyone knows your business. The bar staff have probably seen you walking home from school or they know your parents or siblings.

Getting fake IDs

This was a good option because you would sort of know the places that might not be too fussy about what your ID was but still asked for it. There were all sorts of ways to get hold of one or to fashion your own ID, especially if you knew someone with access to a laminator.

Everyone else turning 18 before you

This was a drag if you were the last one out of all your friends allowed into the pub. There were clever ways around it, though. I remember one pub I couldn't get into (the bouncer knew my sister) but my friends could. I knew the doorman started at 7:30 p.m. so I would have to go down at 7 p.m. and hide upstairs in the toilets until everyone else arrived and someone would come get me from the loo. There were others who climbed in through kitchen windows. We'd do anything not to miss out on the fun.

FUNERAL PINTS

It was only as an adult living abroad that I realised Ireland's funeral etiquette is unique and that each family has their own individual take on it. Death is not something we shy away from. Death, dead, dying. It's not whispered. We aren't afraid of it.

Local radio stations broadcast death notices a few times a day. Most of us will have known a grandparent or parent who listened or still listens. Or perhaps they've moved on to RIP.ie, a website that lists deaths as they are announced. It's a go-to daily check-up for plenty of Irish people of a certain generation – like Facebook but for funerals.

Irish funerals are not the delicate, dressed-in-black events we see in American movies and TV. They are gatherings and are open to all. A wake at home might be a bit more low-key but you usually don't need to be invited and you don't need to dress in black. Anyone can show up, pay their respects, shake hands, share their condolences and depending on who they were to the deceased, be invited for hospitality after.

We have a set of traditions we like to follow, traditions that ground us and bind the bereaved to the dead. Hospitality – and in turn, drink – is a big part of that. Funeral hospitality could have a whole book to itself. It goes back to Brehon Law and Gaelic feasts (see also 'Pints: An origin story'). Providing a decent send-off, including food and drink, was – and still is – expected. We even have a particular style of funeral food: triangle sandwiches, vegetable soup, maybe a carvery. And pints, of course.

> Any home catering is usually informally served tea and triangle-cut sandwiches (egg mayonnaise, or ham, or cheese for vegetarians) along with cakes and scones. Church services are followed by cremation or burial, and the 'afters' now usually take place at a hotel, where that intrinsic Irish hospitality is remnant in the form of a sit-down meal for invited guests. **(*Irish Customs and Rituals* by Dr Marion McGarry)**

The afters, in whatever form, is an important part of the funeral and the grieving process. It offers a welcome distraction – the chance to talk, to reminisce, to share stories and to listen – which is much needed if you're feeling hollow and helpless. Ritually sharing and consuming a pint with someone can be the ideal antidote. In a way, it's the perfect example of why I wanted to write this book. It's not about the drink or the alcohol but rather everything else that surrounds it.

....

Until 1962, publicans were technically obliged to store dead bodies. It was a legal provision that had been brought in under the Coroners Act of 1846, writes Cian Molloy in *The Story of the Irish Pub*: 'Under the Coroners Act of 1846, a coroner could direct that a dead body be brought to the nearest "tavern, public house or house licensed for the sale of spirits" and the owner occupier of such a place was required to allow the body to be kept there until an inquest had taken place.'

It made sense for several reasons: 'Publicans usually had cool storerooms where bodies could be kept from decomposing, and many publicans also ran undertaking businesses.'

....

GUINNESS:
A PINT-SIZED HISTORY

You can't talk about pints without talking about Guinness, one of the best-known beer brands globally. To be honest, it's probably my and many others' favourite pint to drink. In fact, in 2023 Diageo (the Guinness owner) reckoned that more new consumers drank Guinness than ever before. That's quite a feat for a brewery that dates back to 1759 and has essentially been doing the same thing for most of that time.

So why do we love it so much? Well, a short look at its long and storied past, which is as rich as the creamy pint we love, might shed some light on that.

We begin the Guinness story not in Dublin, as most would assume, but in Tipperary in the 1700s. Richard Guinness was a land steward for the Archbishop of Cashel, Rev. Dr Arthur Price. They brewed beer on site and one of Richard's duties was to oversee this. In 1725 Richard's first son was born near Celbridge in Co. Kildare and named Arthur after the archbishop, who then remembered his namesake in his will.

Young Arthur must have spent a bit of time in Cashel, as it seems he caught the bug for brewing, so when the archbishop died and left him £100 in his will, he used the money to set up a small local brewery in Leixlip, Co. Kildare. Four years later, in 1759, Arthur moved things down the road to Dublin, signing a now-legendary 9,000-year lease for a former brewery at St James's Gate in Dublin.

Once set up at St James's Gate, Arthur built up a successful trade. He brewed ales initially but in the 1770s he began experimenting with a darker English beer known as porter. It proved so popular that by 1799, he brewed his last ale and concentrated solely on porter – the early version of the Guinness we drink today. The brewery continued to expand its operations and started exporting to various countries. This global expansion resulted in St James's Gate being the largest brewery in the world by 1880.

By the 20th century, Guinness was a renowned international brand. In 1901 they set up a laboratory to enhance their brewing methods. In 1936 they opened a brewery at Park Royal in London. And on and on. They were – and still are – a forward-thinking company making beer we love to drink.

The Guinness phenomenon

The true phenomenon of Guinness is how it's stayed on top – and even flourished – all these years. It's become an iconic drink, famous around the world. The Guinness Storehouse, a museum dedicated to how the drink is made, is consistently one of the most-visited tourist attractions in Ireland. It was even named the world's leading tourist attraction of 2023 by the World Travel Awards. Guinness has undisputed cult status and has even been enjoying a renaissance of late thanks to all the social media love for this aesthetically pleasing drink.

Along with that social media love, though, there's also been a bit of backlash, as is the norm. People question why a drink as mass-produced as Guinness garners such fanfare, such adoration. It's a fair question. Why is it so revered? Why does it evoke debates at bars all over the world in the same way one might discuss art or fine dining? (See also 'Experts on pints'.)

In Ireland, of course, we think nothing of this. Debating the best Guinness is part and parcel of our culture. It's like talking about the weather. Anyone who drinks Guinness can, and does, have an opinion. It might be their favourite pub, favourite barman or the best glass to serve it in. This is nothing new in Ireland but it did make me wonder how it got to this level. Why do we discuss Guinness, a commercial stout, in the same way sommeliers might debate the great vintages of Château Latour or Château d'Yquem?

There are a myriad of reasons but I reckon it mostly comes down to consistency, not only as a solid and delicious drink but also consistency when it comes to marketing, advertising and a long history of doing good and giving back to the local community. There is goodwill for Guinness in Dublin that has lasted for generations. Even today, when Guinness is owned by a huge global drinks company, Diageo, Ireland still has a sort of spiritual ownership of the brand. Guinness is intrinsically linked to Irish culture.

In addition to this, of course, Guinness has had – and still has – some of the most impressive innovation and marketing ever seen.

Guinness draught and the 'two-part' pour

The ritual of waiting for your Guinness is a quintessential pub experience. It should take exactly 119.5 seconds in total, according to Guinness. You watch the tilted pour, three-quarters of the way up the glass. Then it's placed in your eyeline so you can take in the beauty of the ruby-red stout (yes, red, not black – see page 28) surge and settle. After 60–80 seconds it's topped up, ideally delivering a perfect, slight dome and a creamy head. Divine. The bar person has done their job well. You're grateful for the time and attention your pint gets over the other beers being poured in one go.

For the most part, we don't question the two-part pour. It's a given that Guinness gets more attention. It takes time, we're told. But do you ever wonder if it's not actually 100% necessary to pour your Guinness like this? Have you ever tried it poured in one go, but poured well? Not the one-part sloppy pour that's often the result of a lazy or busy bar, but a slow, consistent pour. Could you tell the difference? Maybe you could. I'm not trying to be controversial here. For the most part, pint pullers and pint drinkers will argue that without the gentle pour and resting time, it won't settle properly. There will be no dome and the head will be sloppy. They swear they will taste and feel the difference. But there are others who claim it's all the same, that the two-part pour is a cod, nothing but a marketing ploy. A barman even told me recently he's heard of people (tourists, mind) requesting a 'straight pour' Guinness. Regardless, I still prefer the two-part pour.

But where did it come from? And why are we so obsessed with it? Turns out there's a solid reason behind it. While Guinness technically dates back to 1759, Guinness draught, the pint of black stuff as we know it now, has only existed since 1959. Prior to that, pouring a pint of Guinness in a pub was even more elaborate than the current two-part pour and the 119.5-second recommended settling time. The early pub system needed two separate kegs of Guinness for the one pint. One keg was fresh and lively, with high pressure, and the other one was older and aged, with low pressure. The high-pressure barrel was poured first, filling the glass with a foamy head. As that settled, the Guinness from the second low-pressure keg, darker and with much fewer bubbles, would be poured to the top. Any excess head or cream was removed and there's your pint. This traditional 'high and low' system was a bit of a hassle and the person pouring really had to have a knack for it, so Guinness, forward-thinking as always, worked on a solution.

In 1951 a mathematician called Michael Ash joined the Guinness team. He discovered that nitrogen was the key to abolishing the two-keg system, and by 1959 Guinness came up with a new way to 'draught' beer with nitrogen. Ever the astute marketers, they launched it to celebrate the 200-year anniversary since Arthur Guinness signed that 9,000-year lease on St James's Gate Brewery. Guinness as we know it was born. It was a huge success locally but it also meant Guinness was much easier to export globally, growing the brand even more.

Even if we technically don't need the two-part pour, I'm good with it. We have enough rushed things in life, enough instant gratification. I want to wait a few seconds longer for my pint and if it makes even the teeniest bit of difference, I'm happy with that. And I'll raise a glass to the man who made pints so consistent and delicious. To Ash!

....

There is a BCC Archive tweet of a video from 1973 of presenter Larry McCoubrey's 'panegyric to porter', where he describes the OG Guinness two-part pour. Here's a snippet of that description, pure pub poetry:

❝ It's drawn from two barrels. A high one first to give it a bit of life. A good glassful of gushing good cheer that settles slowly towards the bottom of the glass into a thick contented cream. It takes several minutes for that cream to substantiate towards the bottom of the glass. When it's ready for the muscle and the sinew, the real body of the drink itself, and that comes from the other barrel of flat. And if it's all drawn properly, the way it should be done, then the cream is born majestically above to form the clerical collar that proves the goodness and its heart. And the true porter drinker would look upon such a glass with great reverence indeed.

....

Guinness advertising and art
Part of how Guinness has continued to build the mystique of the two-part pour is through its impressive advertising and marketing, from famous slogans like 'good things come to those who wait' and 'there's no time like Guinness time' to award-winning television ad campaigns like *Surfer* and *Anticipation*.

Guinness is good for you
Guinness didn't advertise for 170 years, then entered the market in 1929 with the infamous slogan 'Guinness is good for you'. They are of course no longer allowed to use this catchphrase but it lives on in retro Guinness adverts hanging in pubs and restaurants. It also lives on in reputation. People still say 'Guinness is good for you!' in cheers – and let's be honest, to convince ourselves we should have another pint.

John Gilroy
John Gilroy's iconic work for Guinness art is probably the best-known, including his Guinness Zoo campaign, which ran from the 1930s to the 1960s. He is said to have found inspiration for these whimsical illustrations after a trip to the circus with his kids. The designs were characterised by bright colours, playfulness and humour – a concept that simply wouldn't happen today, as it would rightly be thought of as too appealing to children. He also created the famous 'My goodness, my Guinness!' adverts. Gilroy died in 1985 but his artistic legacy lives on. His work is still seen nearly anywhere you find a pint poured, on posters, Guinness collectables, beer mats and plenty more.

The Guinness toucan is always associated with John Gilroy's art but Gilroy wasn't the only one responsible for this iconic imagery. The toucan began his advertising career in the autumn of 1935, when Gilroy worked with copywriter Dorothy L. Sayers. Sayers was a brilliant English poet, novelist, playwright, translator and essayist best known for her best-selling crime fiction, including the Lord Peter Wimsey detective books. Gilroy claimed that he had originally suggested a pelican with a rhyme that was thought inappropriate, so Sayers devised an alternative verse – 'If he can say as you can/Guinness is good for you/How grand to be a Toucan/Just think what Toucan do' – featuring a toucan, which Gilroy duly illustrated.

TV ads

Guinness advertising is well known for being creative, iconic and memorable. TV ads in particular hold a special place in our minds, especially these days, when we're much less likely to see alcohol adverts on TV the way we used to. It's impossible to have the same impact. The old ads are used in university teaching as examples of great work and praised for stunning cinematography and inventive storytelling, often with a hidden deeper meaning or theme. But I mostly remember them because they always made me want to go for a pint. They did their job, so.

Guinness's famous slogan, 'good things come to those who wait', was created in the 1990s to try to turn around the negative consumer opinion about the length of time required to correctly pour a pint of Guinness.

HISTORY OF THE WORLD

(THE IMPORTANT STUFF)

4.5 BILLION YEARS AGO
- EARTH FORMED

1759 AD
- GUINNESS FOUNDED

NOW

ICONIC GUINNESS TV ADVERTS
WITH THE BEST-LOOKING PINTS

Anticipation (1994) Better known as *The Dancing Man*. Actor Joe McKinney dances to 'Guaglione' by Pérez Prado while he waits for his pint of stout to settle, building the anticipation with quirky dance moves. The ad ends with him taking his first, satisfying sip of the freshly poured pint, overlaid by the Guinness slogan 'no time like Guinness time'.

Surfer (1999) You know the one – a moody black-and-white ad with a banging Leftfield soundtrack. A group of surfers waits for the perfect wave, symbolic of the wait for the two-part pour of the perfect Guinness. In 2000 it was named the greatest ad of all time by Channel 4 and has consistently appeared in similar lists since then.

Quarrel (2003) The one where Michael Fassbender swims across the Atlantic to say sorry – and have a few pints, of course. The pints look delicious in it (as does Fassbender) and the soundtrack, 'Heyday' by Mic Christopher, is still as catchy as ever.

As Brian Sibley writes in his book *Guinness Advertising*, 'Guinness has always been the hero of its own advertising, quite simply Guinness advertising has become an institution – like tea, cricket and fish and chips.'

HALF PINTS

'Who's that for, yer ma?'

This, or something similar, might be said to you if you order a half pint in Ireland. But what's the problem? Why do we speak disparagingly of half pints? It's the same beer you're drinking, just half as much. A half pint contains exactly that, half a pint: 284ml, to be precise.

We are so anti-half that you're not even supposed to call it a half. It's usually referred to as a glass, as in 'I'll have a glass of Guinness'. But calling it a glass doesn't mean it fares any better.

Sometimes it even works out more expensive to drink a half (or a glass) than a pint. How unfair is that? Publicans will argue that people stay the same amount of time to drink a half, you still have to wash the glass, etc., but come on, how many people even order halves? And if you're trying to be cautious with the drink or you just don't want a full pint, you should pay more? It doesn't exactly fit the responsible drinking mould.

Why does the half pint get such a hard time? Well, for one thing it's all women were allowed to be served for a long time (see also 'Women, pubs and pints'), so it's already a woman's drink by association.

A friend said recently how annoyed she was that she'd grown up being told it was unladylike to drink a pint. She'd thought of herself as a staunch feminist all these years and then realised she was still ordering glasses of beer in the pub because she had an ingrained belief that as a woman, she shouldn't drink a pint – that it would make her less appealing. It boils my blood to think that there are women going around ordering drinks like this and not according to what they want.

You'd think we'd have left that all behind but I suppose it's not that surprising when you think about how recently women could still be refused a pint in Ireland (technically up until 2000).

Unfortunately it's a stereotype that's still alive in some cohorts. I've seen comments and conversations online around women only ordering pints of Guinness now for 'the gram', with men commenting 'Oh, those poor undrunk pints' when they see them in stylised squares on the internet. I don't see any of them asking a man posting a picture of a pint if he is really drinking it or not.

So I say boo to that. Let's end the gender profiling of drinks and make the half pint cool! A half pint has a time and place and it should be celebrated and well thought of. Maybe you want a lunchtime swiftie, you're running for the bus or you only want a half. Whatever the reason, it doesn't always have to be about the pint. Justice for the half!

JUST A HALF
PINT FOR ME,
CHEERS

HANGOVER PINTS

Hangovers happen to the best of us. If you're lucky, you don't have any plans the day after a feed of pints or that one too many. You can take it easy and get up at your leisure. You can have a big fry-up and endless cups of tea. You can go back to bed. You can watch TV all day. You can plan your OTT takeaway order for later.

But then there are the days when you wake up hungover and the daunting task of having to drink again hangs in the air. Some of us (probably younger ones) can take this in our stride, but the older we get, the harder this gets. The tried-and-tested methods of fixing things are less effective. The Lucozade, Solpadine or Dioralyte don't always do the trick. Sometimes the only thing to do is to have another pint. Sometimes it's even expected of you (wedding day two, holidays, hen parties, weekends away, etc.).

The question is: how do you start? What do you drink? A Bloody Mary often gets touted as the answer – get a shot of vodka and some nutrition into you, then try a pint. If it works for you, fair play. The other option is to just go straight in. Order your pint. Maybe a pint of water or Lucozade first, then go for it. By pint two, you should be feeling okay.

But can a pint the next day fix all woes? Yes and no. But mostly no (sorry). Consuming alcohol dehydrates us and that dehydration is a huge part of the hangovers we suffer. Therefore, having more of what dehydrates us should never be the solution. Why, then, are we so often met with the suggestion of going for a 'hair of the dog'?

A LITTLE BIT OF THE BUBBLY

It's not totally wrong. The full saying is actually 'hair of the dog that bit you', which evolved from the homoeopathic principle *similia similibus curantur*, which loosely means 'like cures like'. So if you were to go down the homoeopathic route, then technically a little of what ails you should fix you. Ergo, a drink should fix your hangover. Well, yes and no again. And mostly no (again, sorry).

While the hair of the dog can be an ideal temporary solution in some situations – like when you're looking into day two of a wedding celebration or you're on holiday with nothing too taxing on the horizon – in general, it's not the best option. Having more drink does not address the underlying issue of dehydration. The hangover is probably still going to be there waiting for you.

There is a sweet spot, though. If you find it, cut yourself off right then and go home. And thank me the next day.

HANGOVER LINGO

- **The cure:** See the hair of the dog above – that drink that promises to fix everything or at least ease the pain.
- **The fear:** An underlying anxiety the day after drinking that is hard to shift.
- **Hangxiety:** Same as the fear.
- **The horrors:** Anxiety plus any other of the many hangover symptoms.
- **In a jock:** This is pretty bad. There's probably vomiting.
- **Sick as a small hospital:** Same as above.
- **Puking my ring up:** There is definitely vomiting.
- **I've an awful head on me:** The headache is bad and not shifting.
- **In rag order:** Feeling bad but probably fixable.
- **In bits:** A flexible one. Could be a worst-case scenario or fixable.
- **In a heap:** As above.
- **In tatters:** As above.
- **I'm dying:** As above.
- **I had a bad pint:** When you don't want to admit you have a hangover (see also 'Bad pints').

HOW TO DRINK
A PINT OF GUINNESS

Much has been written and spoken about how to pour a pint but what about drinking one? The pomp and ceremony don't all belong to the pourer.

If you've spent any time drinking in Irish pubs, even if you aren't a Guinness drinker, you will know what I'm talking about. There is a certain way to correctly imbibe a pint.

The first step is to choose your pub well. If you do that, your pint should be in the preferred glass (old tulip, branded), the pour should be perfect, the domeage, just right. The beer mat corresponds. Then it's over to you.

Get ready. Stand or sit tall. You should drink your pint proudly.

Double check that your pint is settled. There should be a clear division between the creamy head and the black stuff.

Pick up your pint, wrapping your hand around the lower end of the glass. The logos should be both facing you directly and facing out directly.

Your elbow should be straight, lifted 90 degrees from your side. Then lift the glass to your lips and tilt it 45 degrees, making sure you are always looking out to the horizon and never, ever down at your pint. 'Looking to the horizon means you'll take a bigger sip, letting all the flavour in from the dark liquid and the creamy head to get the ideal mix of bittersweet and velvety mouthfeel,' says Pádraig Fox, Global Guinness Ambassador.

Take your first sip, which is really a sup. Make sure you are drinking through the head, not just drinking the head. This is a big mistake that rookies make and it means that first taste will be bitter. The head needs to be drunk with the liquid the whole way down.

A little lick of the lips, a wide smile, and go again. Enjoy each taste as if it were the first of the evening.

Drink from the same side the entire way and take the same size sups. Savour it.

If your pint is good, the head stays more or less the same size the whole way down and the glass will be laced on the far side.

Never, ever drain the glass completely.

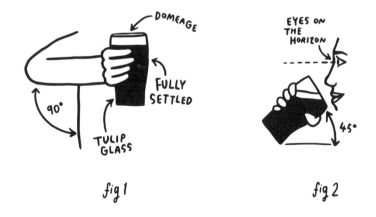

fig 1

fig 2

THE IRISH GOODBYE

We've all done it or perhaps had it done to us – the 'Irish goodbye', leaving the pub/party/ social gathering without actually saying goodbye. You simply up and go, no warning, no word. Just home. You feel a bit wobbly, look at the time and think, 'If I go to the loo and just leg it, I'll feel okay tomorrow.'

To be fair, it's a handy exit to have ready. Saying goodbye in Ireland can be laboursome. Much like our famous welcomes, a goodbye can go on and on and on. We even do it on the phone, no matter how succinct it's meant to be: 'Bye, bye bye bye, bye, bye, bye, bye bye bye, bye, bye so. Bye, bye bye.'

In the pub, it's even riskier. Someone might get you another drink, you get pulled back into a conversation, your rubber arm appears and next thing you know you've had a shot and you're off dancing. It's often better just to take your leave when you can.

The origin of the term, though, is not so wonderous. It's most likely rooted in 19th-century stereotypes about the Irish in America, which were less than favourable. This is also likely why it seems like a much more popular term in the US than there in Ireland. There are other variants of this ethnophobic term too, including 'the Dutch leave', while back in the day the English would have called it 'the French leave' and the French reciprocated with *filer à l'anglaise*, literally 'to dash off English style'.

But no matter where it came from, there's no denying it's a great tactic to have up your sleeve. Sometimes it's the politest way to go. Maybe it's time to reclaim if for ourselves.

THE IRISH PUB

❝ Ireland is synonymous with pubs. Traditionally, the pub was the focal point of community life. For some, alcohol encouraged joyful moments, an emigration of the soul from sometimes unhappy realities. But for most people, the pub was there for sheer delight. You never knew who you'd meet, or what strange wisdom someone might pass on. Ideas rebounded from the tobacco-stained walls into every snug and cranny; giddy fiddles and rattling tongues could enliven the darkest corners. **(Fennell and Bunbury, 2008)**

This book is an ode to the pint, not the pub, but what is a pint without the pub? They can technically exist without each other but it's their coexistence that makes them what they are. A pint without a pub is like a Jedi without the Force, a pen without paper, a driver without a car. They need each other. They are infinitely better together. So allow me, then, to wax lyrical about the pub for a while. But not just any pub – the OG, the Big Kahuna, the grand game/duke, the greatest of them all: the Irish Pub.

❝ We speak today of 'the Irish pub' as if it is something knowable and distinct, a singular space albeit with multitudinous manifestations, but which share a readily identified commonality of traits and which serve as a unifying marker of Irishness where they are found. **(Carrigy, 2019)**

What is the Irish pub?
The strictest definition of an Irish pub may just be a pub in Ireland, pub being short for public house, which refers to a drinking establishment

licensed to serve alcoholic drinks for consumption on the premises. But the real definition of what makes it an Irish pub, a *proper* pub, is far more nuanced.

The Irish pub is not just a pub in Ireland, but a specific *type* of pub in Ireland. We may also call it 'a traditional pub', 'an old man's pub' (pages 130–1), 'a pint pub', 'a Guinness pub' or even just 'a proper pub'. Try it. Ask anyone in Ireland where the nearest proper pub is and they'll know what you mean and direct you there with a knowing nod. To even begin to define it in specifics might be too much, so what might work better is to list some of the characteristics we expect from the Irish pub (and then some we don't – see also 'Keltic pints').

It should be old

It should be old – preferably at least 100 years old. It should also be unchanged as much as possible, with bonus points for any original fittings or any relics of the past, such as a Victorian ceiling, flagstone floors, cabinets full of curios, brass bar taps, ornate mirrors or stained glass that has lasted the course. The main claim to the title of oldest pub in Ireland is Sean's Bar in Athlone, which dates all the way back to 900 AD.

It should have authentic décor

As above, the pub should be old and the décor should be as authentic as possible. In some cases that could mean grand wood panelling or ornate stained glass windows. You'll often still see the ceilings and walls covered in Lincrusta, a hard-wearing covering with embossed patterns.

But it can also be a chequered linoleum floor or random grocery shelves full of tea, lightbulbs and tinned fruit. It can be a cast iron fireplace. There could be piles of eclectic pub paraphernalia. Maybe postcards and different currencies are tacked up on the ceiling. There could be a gallery wall of black-and-white photographs. Whatever the décor, it should be timeworn and only exist because someone else put it there.

    ❝ Despite the temptation to change décor over the years, these old pubs have remained largely unchanged from when they first opened in the 19th or early 20th century. In terms of furniture and interior design, they define what an Irish pub should be in decorative terms. **(McGarry, 2023)**

There is likely a lot of wood inside – panelling, perhaps; dark, old and original – and mirrors featuring forgotten whiskey brands. If there's a snug (see also pages 172–4), it's small with uncomfortable seats but it's still the most coveted spot in the bar. If there's a fire, it should be lit, even in the summer. Or maybe there's a Superser heater plugged in.

There should have been little to no improvements made over the years, and if there have been any they should be purely practical. We're not adverse to the pubs that have added a ladies' toilet. That's an adjustment we welcome.

    ❝ Particular types of older pubs are even more important and could be argued to represent living cultural heritage. Those that have largely retained their original shopfronts and interiors to such an extent that they can act almost as interactive museums. If your grandfathers or uncles supped in them – or you reckon that they did – you can imagine their past by experiencing these places. **(McGarry, 2023)**

Simply put, they are living museums.

It should have a quiet atmosphere

For the most part, and particularly during the day, it should be quiet and solemn. Many pubs will have no music on, ever, except perhaps for a live trad session. Some might have one TV tucked away turned on for the big racing days or an All-Ireland. If there is chat, it might be orchestrated by the bar staff and a local sitting at the bar with a crossword or a folded-up newspaper. It could be a few words. It could be about the weather, the match or the price of things going up. The evenings might get louder with chat, but they are not often rowdy.

There should be a particular kind of service

Don't expect any fanfare upon entering. In fact, if you feel a bit like you're intruding or like you're getting sized up, it's because you are. There is an imbalance of power here. The bar staff are in charge and you should quietly accept that. In a real pub, there should be no fussy *céad míle fáilte*. A nod and a 'what are you having' is perfectly welcoming. You're expected to order something straightforward. Once you and your pint have settled, there may be an option for conversation. If you're open to it, in no time you'll be figuring out if you have a cousin in common, if they know your uncle or if you went to the same caravan park years ago. Common ground and chat are important currency in the proper pub.

....

The Irish Pub: FILM This 2013 documentary by Alex Fegan is a must-watch for any Irish pub enthusiasts. It captures the changing face of traditional Irish pubs, showing them just as they are in their simplest form, and still, it elevates them. Candid chats with publicans and locals provide a remarkable snapshot of pub history.

....

The Irish Pub: BOOK Published in 2008, The Irish Pub is a collaboration of photography by James Fennell and writing by historian Turtle Bunbury. It showcases 39 classic pubs around Ireland with stunning photographs of perfect moments in time – simple images of wooden snugs, flat caps, leather stools and pints, of course.

....

The Irish Pub – UNESCO site of Intangible Cultural Heritage?

Irish pubs are much more than just boozers and our love for them is about more than just nostalgia. And I'm not the only one who thinks so. Recently there has been some promising chat about the possibility of Irish pubs becoming protected as UNESCO sites of Intangible Cultural Heritage.

I first came across this idea thanks to Róisín Murphy, an Irish conservation architect who believes we are guilty of overlooking 'the very vernacular Irish architecture and culture'. In 2023 she presented a documentary on RTÉ, Róisín Murphy's Big City Plan, focusing on the derelict and vacant buildings in Ireland's towns and cities, highlighting how we don't always perceive everyday Ireland and rural Ireland as 'heritage', our pubs included.

I interviewed her for a *Sunday Times* Ireland article I wrote in 2023, where she said,

> ❝ The Irish pub seems like an innocuous, almost quaint thing, but it's actually a very important piece of cultural reference. As they disappear from the Irish countryside you realise that there is something more that's going with it – it's an intangible heritage we are losing.

Our pubs are full of this 'invisible culture'. While talking about it in a previous interview, Murphy suggested that traditional Irish pubs could be protected as UNESCO sites of Intangible Cultural Heritage. This struck a chord with many.

The Vintners' Federation of Ireland (VFI) has since made a submission to the Department of Culture in regard to pubs joining the list of the National Inventory of Intangible Cultural Heritage of Ireland. The VFI cite 'a sense of community, conviviality, and kinship' along with the old origins of the Irish pub as reasons why they should be considered. There was even talk from the Oireachtas Tourism Committee that we could audit rural areas and find potential candidates for a UNESCO list. Meanwhile, the VFI awaits a response from UNESCO.

It's too early to know if this could be a solution but it's certainly getting people talking and that can only be a good thing.

JUST THE ONE

A cousin of unplanned pints (see also pages 192–3), 'just the one' can be a hero or a villain depending on how it goes.

It's a hero when you really do mean it and you just go for one. You get that sweet release of going for a pint but you still go about your day or your evening as planned. You still get your bits done and wake up fresh the next day. When it's executed well, it can be joyous. However, there are obstacles to overcome.

Just the one (each)

A safe in-between place is when you go for just the one but just the one means two. This happens when you're only with one other person, so each person gets to buy just the one. It's risky because giddiness can set in at any moment and before you know it, one becomes three. But if you can stick to just one each (so two, really), you're still in a good place and can reap the benefits of your discipline.

The sneaky pint buyer

There will be someone who won't believe you when you say you're going for 'just the one', someone you know wants to stay out for more. You'll need to avoid them. Do not engage. Even if you avoid them, watch out because they will go to the bar when you aren't looking and order you another. Depending on how rubbery your arm is, you can stay or go.

Transport timings

'Oh no, I won't, my train is due.' Or maybe you've to be home for dinner or similar. But this excuse can also be used to sneak in another: 'My next bus isn't due for 20 minutes, may as well.' This is a slippery slope, though. Next thing you know, you're swaying on the platform, squinting at the departure times and wishing you'd eaten.

Go on, go on, go on

We all know a Mrs Doyle. They insist. Insist again. And will be highly insulted if you say no. It's usually just easier to have another.

Yourself

Sometimes you only have yourself to blame. You take that first sip and it tastes like more. You get the goo. You can't help it. You know you're going to have another. And maybe another. Crisps for dinner it is, then (see also 'Crisps and pints').

CRISPS FOR DINNER?

YES!

I'LL HAVE 2-5 PACKETS PLEASE

KELTIC PINTS

Are Irish pubs our greatest export? Just like McDonald's, there are few places in the world where you won't find an Irish pub. We see them on every city break or beach holiday we go on, in obscure American cities and in far-flung destinations. They have a similar appeal to Maccy D's – you should always get what you expect: a typical Irish pub with an 'Oirish' welcome, Guinness on tap, wood panelling and knick-knacks.

Yet the Irish pub is not as easy to replicate as the Golden Arches. Although people try all around the globe, an Irish pub that is not in Ireland will simply never hit the mark like a pub at home. Note: There is a distinct difference between Irish-Irish pubs and Irish-themed pubs. Let me elaborate.

Irish-Irish pubs

There are Irish pubs around the world that are owned, set up and/or run by Irish people. These are the ones to seek out. While they may still have a hint of Darby O'Gill about them, the pint is probably poured well and there is a chance of some Irish bar staff.

You'll find them in Moscow, Nepal, Argentina and Mongolia. The one that's said to be the furthest away from Ireland is the Bog in Dunedin, New Zealand. In the US they seem to be in every city, and in the 'Irish' cities like New York, Chicago and Boston you'll likely find an Irish bar in every borough.

These don't have to be bars that scream, 'I'm Irish!' Sometimes you'll know just by the beer they serve. When I first left home at 17 and moved to a Greek island for the summer, our first stop (along with the rest of the Irish) was the Fun Pub, a Greek-owned bar run by a Dubliner called Mick Burke. They had a Guinness sign out front, so that was Irish enough for us. That summer and the next ones we spent in Greece, the Fun Pub became our unofficial embassy. That was where our post was sent and where our parents could call us (these were the days before mobiles and email). It's where we went to ask if there were any jobs going or when we needed advice.

Irish-Irish pubs abroad are more than just a place to have a drink or watch a match with fellow fans. They can act as de facto embassies and employment offices. They are a link to other Irish people and an instant community.

Sure, we might roll our eyes at some of the names (The Keltic! The Fun Pub!) or cringe at the OTT 'Oirish' paraphernalia on display, but we'll still seek them out for familiarity, friendship and hopefully a decent pint. Irish-Irish pubs are a home away from home.

Irish-themed pubs
These are a different kettle of fish – cut-and-paste replicas of Irish pubs that have been built all over the world, no Irish heritage necessary. There is even a business called the Irish Pub Company that has been exporting 'Irish pubs' since 1990. At last count, they claim to be responsible for over 2,000 Irish pubs worldwide in over 60 countries.

This design-and-build firm specialises in creating an Irish pub concept and builds it for you, incorporating traditional Irish elements like the woodwork, bar stools, décor and of course pub paraphernalia. I've not been to many so I can't really comment, but I imagine that you need more than dark wood, the Dubliners playing on a loop and Guinness on tap to capture the essence of a real-deal Irish pub. Yet Dr Marion McGarry, writing about

exported Irish pubs for RTÉs *Brainstorm*, suggests some are done so well that we might not notice the difference:

> The unique character of traditional Irish pub interiors has led to them becoming one of our most successful design exports. Irish pubs in all corners of the globe mimic these older interiors and many contemporary pub fit out companies operate 'turn key' refurbishment services that do 'traditional' so well many think they are original.

New Age Irish pubs

The latest generation of diaspora, however, is offering something different. A 2023 *Irish Times* article by Una Mullally showcased New York Irish bars that are 'pushing the boundaries of Irish culture'.

They included Copper Johns in Midtown Manhattan, opened by Conor Myers from Dundalk and Archie Dolan from Darndale in Dublin, whom Mullally says were 'keen to create a pub with a sense of Irishness', adding, 'The pair plan to avoid the usual tropes. Instead, the focus will be on contemporary Irish heritage, with Irish street art, Irish street photography, artwork drawn from Irish rave flyers, and a soundtrack of Irish music that reflects the vibrant Irish traditional, rock, and hip-hop scene back home.'

She also chatted to Dubliner Ryan Skelton about his Ibiza-inspired discoteca, Cafe Balearica in Williamsburg, New York, and Kerry native Brenda Breathnach, who runs 3 Dollar Bill, a huge LGBTQ+ nightclub.

Leading the way in New York, of course, is the Dead Rabbit. At this Irish pub they 'celebrate the pubs of home, classic and contemporary cocktails, and the modern Irish maker'. And they just so happen to hold the title of the most awarded bar in the world.

It's no wonder everyone wants a piece of the Irish pub.

It's important to note that proximity to Ireland usually means a better Irish pub. The same goes for if there is a big Irish diaspora in an area. It's not guaranteed that every pub will be good but there should be an Irish pub that's approved by the Irish if a lot of them live there.

THE WORLD'S BEST IRISH PUB
(OUTSIDE IRELAND)

The most authoritative list I could find was from 2015, when the *Irish Times* launched a competition to search for the world's best Irish pub (outside Ireland) as part of the *Irish Times* Generation Emigration project, a section of the irishtimes.com website devoted to Irish people overseas. Over the course of a month, more than 1,500 people in 41 countries wrote in to vote for their favourite Irish pub outside Ireland (Goodman, 2015).

The final top 10 pubs selected were:
- The Auld Shillelagh, London, UK
- Bubbles O'Leary, Kampala, Uganda
- The Drunken Poet, Melbourne, Australia
- Finn McCool's, New Orleans, US
- Healy Macs, Kuala Lumpur, Malaysia
- The Irish Haven, New York, US
- Irish Pub Koblenz, Germany
- The Irish Times, Vancouver Island, Canada
- The James Joyce, Prague, Czech Republic
- The Wild Rover hostel in Cusco, Peru

THE LOCAL

When you first start drinking, you'll likely choose the pub you can get served in or the pub someone you know drinks in. When you move away from home, unhindered by your shackles, you can usually pick any pub to be your local.

But why do we want a local so badly? What is it that's so appealing about walking into a pub where someone knows your name and your drink? Did we watch too many episodes of *Cheers* growing up?

It's not just *Cheers*. Irish TV had plenty of locals too. There was Teasy McDaid's pub on *Glenroe* and McCoy's on *Fair City*. The UK soaps had more dramatic locals, which were often at the epicentre of the biggest storylines: the Rovers Return on *Coronation Street*, the Woolpack on *Emmerdale* and the infamous Queen Vic on *Eastenders*.

One of the most famous pieces of writing about a local pub is George Orwell's 1946 essay 'The Moon Under Water', originally published as the Saturday Essay in the London paper the *Evening Standard*. In the essay he listed the qualities possessed by this wonderous pub, only to reveal at the end that the pub did not exist – he'd wished it into being.

Now I'm no Orwell, but I also have a list of things I expect from a local. The local that we yearn for even if we've never had a local. The place we'd walk into and say, 'It feels like a real local.' But to be honest his list was so spot on that it only needs a few edits to be brought up to date for modern-day Ireland.

Consists mostly of 'regulars' and staff know customers by name This is still an essential. Although I don't mind if they don't know my name, they should at least pretend to or acknowledge that I've been there before.

....

Victorian interiors Or as Orwell said, 'everything has the solid, comfortable ugliness of the 19th century'. Shiny new pubs don't make great locals. The older, the better.

....

A good fire burning Yes, please. Bonus if there's a newspaper.

....

Quiet enough to talk (no music) Agreed!

....

Snacks available Ideally a simple toastie, old-school crisps and Scampi Fries (see also 'Toasties and pints' and 'Crisps and pints').

....

Draught stout Goes without saying.

....

Particular about their drinking vessels Beers in the correct glasses and nice and clean, please (see also 'The pint glass').

....

Beer garden A summer essential.

....

Women are welcomed Luckily we don't have to state this anymore.

....

If you really want an insight into what a local pub should be and has been, there's a wonderful documentary called *The Irish Pub* that encapsulates the feeling of a local better than I can on paper (see also page 109).

LOCK-IN PINTS

The lock-in is a quintessential Irish pub experience but it's not the easiest one to find, probably because of the legal ambiguity around them. A lock-in occurs when the pub allows you to stay and continue drinking after closing time. To simply stay open and serve would be illegal but closing the doors and hosting a 'private party' with 'friends' is not. Or so I've been told. At many a lock-in.

How you end up at a lock-in is also ambiguous. Most likely you're a local, you know a local or you know the owner or someone who works there. If you're selected, you'll only know by a look, a nod or a whisper. Then there is a particular dance that has to happen to empty the rest of the pub. Not an actual dance, but rather an excruciating period of time from when the rest of the punters are turfed out. 'Are you right there folks please?' is called from the bar to signal that it's time to go. But you haven't been asked to leave. You're sitting there pretending not to be excited that you're allowed to stay, trying to make the end of your pint last. Perhaps you're even hidden in a back bit and have been told to keep quiet. All of this is building up to that first sweet sip of your illicit lock-in pint.

Then it happens. The doors are closed. Latched. You're locked in. Blinds are pulled down. Some lights are turned off. Anything to minimise attention from outside. It used to be the case that the ashtrays would come out, even after the smoking ban, but that's less common now. Someone appears behind the bar. The pints start to be poured. Bliss.

Pints are the name of the game here. No one wants to be faffing around after hours making complicated drinks. And most important of all, if no money is passing over the bar to keep things 'legal', pints are the easiest things for the bar to write off as 'spillage'.

A lock-in might be a few quiet ones or it may turn out to be a more raucous affair. There could be sing-songs, heated debate, a guitar, dancing on bars and more. It all depends. You'll never know. And that's the great thing about lock-in pints, a pub's worst-kept secret.

HOW TO GET THE NOD FOR A LOCK-IN

- Be a local or befriend a local.
- Be a pint drinker! Easier all round.
- Be a nice customer, civilised, polite, make chat, tip and buy the bar staff a drink. Then ask them what happens after closing...
- Be a celebrity. Margot Robbie and Jimmy Fallon are among the celebrities who have boasted about being at Irish lock-ins.
- Don't ever ask if there's a lock-in.

MATCHMAKING AND PINTS

Pints and pubs have a particular place in the romantic lives of Irish people and have done for a long time. For centuries before we could swipe right, suitors could be found via a local matchmaker. A third-party, sort of semi-professional would negotiate a pairing, a dowry, etc. in the 19th and even early 20th century, and guess where they often operated from? Pubs, of course. Pubs – and snugs in particular – could act as meeting places for discussions and set-ups. There were even some publicans who ran a side-line in matchmaking.

Pubs have always provided space for pursuing and approaching romantic interests. The clichéd Dutch courage (that could be renamed Irish courage!) has contributed many a helping hand to relationships, situationships and romantic successes (and disasters, of course).

But what place do pints and pubs have in modern matchmaking? Pubs can still play an important role in romantic endeavours. The pub is still a good place to meet people. If you pick the right spot, it could be brimming with potential. Getting chatting to someone by 'bumping' into them at the bar or asking them for a light in the smoking area are tried-and-tested methods. Remember when 'smirting' (smoking and flirting) was all the rage when smoking areas first appeared (see also 'No smoking: Pints and cigarettes')? Fewer people smoke now but I suppose these days you might compare notes on vape flavours? Or turn on a dating app and see who's in your vicinity. The point is to pick the right place. There's still nowhere else you can potentially be surrounded by so many singletons.

But where does the pint fit into all this? We have cafés and coffeeshops galore now, but they are still relatively new spaces and not somewhere many of us head to with love on our minds. The same goes for wine bars and cocktail bars. They don't have the same casual, I-could-chat-with-you-for-hours vibes that pubs have. The pub, and in turn, pints, are a safer bet.

Pints are also a great leveller. There's no complicated drink to be chosen, shaken or made, then sipped from a tall or dinky glass. A pint is just a pint.

What about when you've made a match and a date is on the cards? We've romanticised them enough in literature over the years (see also 'Pints, pubs and poets'), but is it romantic to have a pint on a date? Yes! Even if you don't necessarily want to drink pints on the date, if someone asks you out for pints, it means they want a chat. It's open-ended and it's full of possibilities. Anything could happen! What's not to love about that?

But there are still many things to consider. When it comes to picking a pub, do you choose somewhere you know? Somewhere cool? Or somewhere nondescript? Do you get there first? If you are first, do you order the other person a pint? Do you text them and ask what they're having? And if you're the person who's being texted, what do you say? So many variables, but still fewer than going for cocktails or dinner.

If you're in the pub and have the luck of witnessing a couple's first pint, you might just get to watch two people fall head over heels. Or you might get to witness the absolute awkwardness of two people realising that their frenzied texting doesn't translate into a spark in real life. Either way, it's entertaining.

NO SMOKING: CIGARETTES AND PINTS

'A cigarette is the perfect type of a perfect pleasure. It is exquisite, and it leaves one unsatisfied. What more can one want?' That's Oscar Wilde making cigarettes sound delectable in *The Picture of Dorian Gray*. Remember when so many of us thought that they were? We'd light up in all sorts of places. Offices, airplanes, shops, cafés, restaurants, languidly smoking between meals, between phone calls, on phone calls. And in pubs. For many, a pint wasn't a pint without a smoke. But can you even imagine smoking in a pub now?

It's been a while. Ireland made history in March 2004 when a workplace smoking ban was enforced, which included pubs and restaurants. We were the first country in the world to do so. Overnight, thousands of ashtrays were made redundant as smoking in enclosed workplaces became illegal, punishable by a fine of up to €3,000. There was outrage and protests from many publicans and smokers predicting it would be last orders for Irish pubs, but it went ahead regardless. While it certainly wasn't the end of the pub, it did herald some big changes in the pub culture in Ireland.

Smoking and pints in pubs were bed buddies for a long time. It makes sense – they work similarly, both releasing dopamine into your body. Lighting up that first pub cigarette is akin to your first sip of the first cold pint. Lots of people would never have one without the other. And pubs catered to smokers. If you hadn't stocked up on cigarettes before the pub, you'd buy them from the creaky cigarette vending machine hanging on the wall that often took three goes to work, spitting your change out at you. There were ashtrays on every table, usually heavy brown glass ones. There were boxes of matches behind the bar or matchbooks with the pub name or logo on them for you to take home. It was a genius bit of marketing that is no more. Pub staff had to do laps of tables all day and night changing ashtrays, dumping the piles of cigarette butts into a bucket as they went.

When the smoking ban came in, the most noticeable thing was the change in the smell. Smokeless pubs were stinky. The natural smell of a pub was not something we were prepared for. Without the daily dousing of tobacco, all the other odours were allowed to combine and rise up to meet us – in carpeted pubs in particular. The leftover stench of sticky spilled drinks, the bodies and bottoms that had filled the pub the night before, burps, puke, wafts from the toilet and even the cleaning chemical smells were new to us. In those early days of the ban, an unmasked smoke-free pub hit hard. We're used to it now, though. Have pubs adjusted or have we?

So what did we do? Some people gave up smoking, which of course was what the ban was hoping to achieve. Some people stayed home and drank, disgusted that they could no longer puff away as they pleased, but the lure of the pub eventually proved to be too much. Pouring your own cans just isn't the same, as we well know (see also 'Cans vs. pints').

We didn't desert the pubs completely. The pubs adjusted to suit the ban. All over the country, forgotten outdoor areas were embraced. Ashtrays and stools were added to alleyways and outdoor keg storage spots. Purpose-built shelters and outdoor seating flew up. Some were what could only be described as smoking emporiums, as savvy pub owners tweaked and bent the rules so much that there were (and still are) pubs and nightclubs where the only way you can tell you're outside is by the waft of tobacco, not by any other outdoor element. Pubs without any outdoor space had to figure out how to control the crowds gathering on footpaths outside, swaying into the streets.

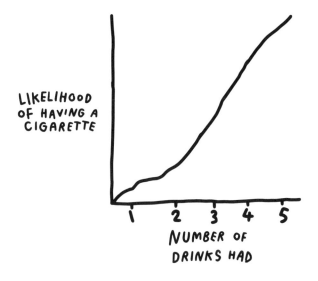

The smoking areas became the place to be. Non-smokers would brave the wintry weather so as not to miss out on the *craic*. Forget speed dating – the smoking area was where you headed to strike up a conversation and do a bit of smirting. Sparks still fly there in more ways than one.

THE OLD MAN'S PUB

On a visit to Westport, Co. Mayo, I wanted to go for a tasty Saturday afternoon pint. You know the kind, with a few packets of crisps to stave off the hunger before dinner. I posed the question to a few local hospitality folks: 'Where should I go for a nice pint?'

Someone replied with a pub I'd heard of. 'You'd like it, it's cosy.'

Another suggestion was followed with, 'It's lovely and buzzy.'

I knew neither of them would hit the spot. Cosy, maybe, but buzzy? No, thanks. I needed to be more specific.

'Any old man's pubs? You know, with a good pint?'

The young barman from Sligo knew just the spot. 'Moran's,' he said. 'Johnny Moran's is the one. They do a great pint of Guinness in there.' That sealed the deal.

It was the least assuming of the busy Westport pub facades but inside it was picture-perfect. Black-and-white chequered floors. A sort of grocery on one wall, full of non-perishables, dog food, toilet rolls and TK lemonade. Haphazard shelves behind the bar tacked with currency notes from around the world. Bottles of whiskey in no particular order. The few people sitting at the bar turned, looked us up and down, then ignored us. Johnny Moran himself was behind the bar and poured us a pleasant set of pints. We stayed for three.

There's a knack to finding these pubs – the proper pubs, the 'old man's pubs'. Most towns in Ireland still have one. The key to seeking them out is to ask specifically for an old man's pub or an auld lad's pub, depending on where you are. No bells and whistles, no noisy music or fancy food. A no-nonsense pub. A well-poured pint. Maybe a few packets of crisps. What more could you want? (See also 'The Irish pub'.)

OUTDOOR PINTS

You know what it's like when you get a glimpse of summer in Ireland. Sure, where else would you want to be? It's not just great for drying but great for pints too. When the sun is splitting the stones, especially midweek, it simply feels rude not to go for a pint. If you've been in any city centre when the good weather hits, you'll be familiar with the sight of people pouring out onto pavements, sitting on kerbs, standing in groups blocking footpaths and altogether delighted with themselves. When the sun shines, we will sit, stand or perch anywhere there's no shade. And when a proper heatwave hits, it's beer garden frenzy. We can't get to the pub quickly enough, nabbing picnic tables soon to be littered with empty glasses and the sunscreen we forget to put on.

An rud is annamh is iontach, as they say (what's rare is wonderful). Because let's face it, the dry, sunny weather that suits outdoor pints is not always guaranteed in Ireland, which is why we go so crazy for it when it happens.

For the most part, outdoor seating is still a relatively new addition to Irish pubs. The traditional pub was all about dark interiors, cosy corners, snugs and carpets. It wasn't the done thing to head to the pub and seek a seat outside. But a few things changed this in the last couple of decades. The smoking ban (see also pages 127–9) meant publicans rethought outdoor spaces they'd never considered. More recently, the covid lockdowns in 2020 and 2021 forced pubs to think outside the box – quite literally – when they couldn't do business indoors. It's one of the few silver linings from that dark time for pubs. Car parks were repurposed into cool new

seating areas, terraces were transformed and benches appeared on any bit of grass that might be around. We've now got outdoor spaces galore for sipping pints.

Best of all are the pubs that are known for their outdoor seating, rain or shine. Pints in these coveted seats are special – soaking up a city or people watching. It's a vibe. Cheers to the outdoor pints.

OYSTERS AND PINTS

When I say oysters and pints, I specifically mean stout. And when I say stout, I mean Guinness. It's a classic food pairing that has been a thing since at least 1837, when Benjamin Disraeli, the future Prime Minister of the UK, wrote to his sister telling her about an impressive food pairing he'd had at the opening of Queen Victoria's first Parliament, where he tried oysters and Guinness and declared it 'the most remarkable day hitherto of my life'. High praise indeed.

In modern times, Guinness might have shared his quote on their socials or sent Disraeli a press drop of Guinness and oysters. They didn't do nothing, of course – it's Guinness! One hundred years later, they published an ad in *Time* magazine featuring Disraeli's quote. Ads and posters declared them a perfect match from then on, along with 'Guinness and oysters are good for you'. You'll even find reference to it in the Guinness Storehouse in Dublin, where they have a restaurant called 1837 inspired by the Disraeli quote, serving Guinness and oysters, of course.

Disraeli was not wrong – it's a remarkable pairing. The slightly bitter, sweet-tasting stout goes great with the briny flesh of an oyster. To this day, tourists come to Ireland seeking out the quintessential oysters-and-stout experience, in particular at the Galway International Oyster and Seafood Festival that happens every September (the start of oyster season!). There's always plenty of Guinness, Murphy's and the rest flowing that week.

Another curious connection oysters have to pints is in the brewing process. Have you ever had an oyster stout and wondered what the

oyster bit referred to? It's not just that they go great with oysters – oyster shells were once used as a filtration method to refine and clarify beers. Modern oyster stouts, though, use other methods of clarification and oysters are used in different capacities in the brewing process to add that unique briny flavour.

PADDY'S DAY PINTS

St Patrick's Day – or Paddy's Day, as we usually call it (never, ever Patty's!) – is the most famous Irish occasion when pints are consumed around the world. It's technically a holy day to honour our patron saint, St Patrick, best known for spreading Christianity throughout Ireland during the 5th century. Oh, and for getting rid of the snakes too. The day itself has been observed since around the 10th century, with the first official feast day taking place in 1631.

It's a giddy time of year. Spring is coming after a dark winter. Then March 17th, St Patrick's Day, arrives, a global celebration that usually makes people think of a day-long party with everyone in the pub, sinking green beers, knocking back sticky shots and wearing leprechaun hats. Paddy's Day is like that friend who has a reputation for always having a good time – the one who will buy a round of shots too early, convince you to stay out and will have you dancing on the bar and forgetting that you ever did so.

The reality of St Patrick's Day (in Ireland, anyway) is more nuanced than that. Yes, we celebrate, and yes, some of us go to the pub, but it always feels like the rest of the world and the tourists who flock to Ireland for the day are having a much madder time than us. With every St Patrick's Day that passes, Ireland is successfully inching further away from booze being the central part of it.

So where does the party reputation come from? The date it falls on, March 17th, is probably the first thing that plays a role in the party vibe. St Patrick's Day usually occurs halfway through Lent, the Catholic

PADDY'S DAY IN DUBLIN

POOLBEG   SILLY HAT   CRAP PINT   PUDDLE OF
PISS

observance of prayer and fasting for 40 days before Easter, when people choose to abstain from things as a sign of sacrifice and to test their self-discipline. In effect, St Patrick's Day is considered a day off from Lent. When we were kids we were expected to give up sweets and treats for Lent, so St Patrick's Day was a big deal. It was a chance to eat something lovely — sweets from the shop or maybe a green ice cream. For adults, it meant you could reach for a drink. It's human nature — take something away from us and we'll want it more.

The fact that up until 1973 you couldn't even go to the pub on St Patrick's Day in Ireland was another factor, as Dr Marion McGarry writes in her book *Irish Customs and Rituals*:

" Lore has it that until then, the only legal place to get a drink in Ireland was within the Royal Dublin Society Dog Show. In the years that the pubs were closed in Ireland, people still found ways around the ban to consume alcohol. They tended to celebrate at gatherings in their homes or the local 'rambling house'. The alcohol consumed on St Patrick's Day was known as *Póta Phádraig* or 'St Patrick's Pot'. The tradition known as 'drowning the shamrock' involves making a toast to St Patrick then tossing a shamrock over the shoulder for good luck (most convenient considering that adults wore bunches of shamrock on their lapels). The shamrock was unpinned, placed in the last drop of alcohol, then when the toast was drunk removed from the glass and tossed over the shoulder.

So booze has long been a part of the day. But what about the parades? It turns out they're a result of the Irish Temperance movement trying to stop us boozing — again. McGarry tells us:

" Because of the association with alcohol, the day became a focus for the Irish Temperance movement, which was an anti-alcohol, religious association that exemplified good behaviour and national pride. From the mid-nineteenth century, they held colourful parades on St Patrick's Day which offered a celebratory teetotal alternative to alcohol pursuits. These parades spread to Irish emigrant communities abroad and they became embedded in the international celebration of St Patrick's Day and brought it to a global audience.

So we have the Temperance movement to thank for the parades but probably more so the Irish diaspora (see also pages 69–70), who have made St Patrick's Day such a global phenomenon. The parades are now a big part of the celebrations. You'll find flashy versions all over the world but the best are still the authentic home parades that take place in every town and village across Ireland, with tractors, Irish dancing and local GAA teams marching proudly. Pints always optional.

A FEW OTHER NOTES ON ST PATRICK'S DAY PINTS

- It's Paddy's Day – *never* Patty's Day!
- We don't dye our pints or our rivers green.
- We don't put shamrocks on our pints of stout (well, maybe for tourists).
- We don't all spend the day in the pub, but if we do, we have a good reason (see above).

THE PINT GLASS

Branded pint glasses

Have you ever been served Guinness in the wrong glass? Or your Bulmers in a Smithwick's glass? Ugh. It gives me the ick just writing it. There's nothing wrong with the drinks as such; no doubt they taste the same. But it's just not proper. Your pint should co-ordinate with your glass. Right?

This may be a particularly Irish thing. People in other places will happily drink a beer from any glass as long as it's cold and wet. They're not concerned that the logo emblazoned across their glass doesn't match what's in it. And why should they be? It doesn't actually make a difference.

But it does! To me, and to lots of other Irish people.

I remember the detail with which I learned correct glass etiquette in my first pub job: always put the right drink in the right branded glass. The shelves were even organised as such, lined with criss-crossed plastic glass mats so that the glass would be raised up from the wood to dry. There was also a particular system of restocking the shelves so that you would never use a glass still warm from the washer.

When you poured a Guinness, you used a Guinness glass. Smithwick's went into a pint glass with the word Smithwick's and the little castle logo on it. Harp (it was the 1990s – see page 37) went through a few glass styles, but you'd always put your Harp in a Harp glass.

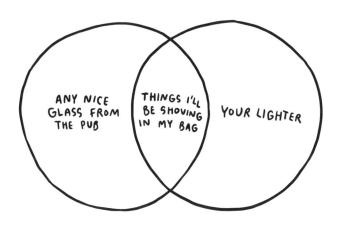

ANY NICE GLASS FROM THE PUB

THINGS I'LL BE SHOVING IN MY BAG

YOUR LIGHTER

There might be a stash of unmarked pint glasses you could use if you ran out of the correct branded one, but you NEVER poured a Guinness in a Smithwick's glass or vice versa. Even the plain pint glasses had a hierarchy. You used the tulip style first and the nonic (stackable) ones only if you were desperate.

Judith Boyle, publican and lecturer in beverages, says we have Guinness (Diageo) to thank for this. Ever since they deployed quality control teams to Irish pubs to make sure things are done right, the importance of the correct branded glass has been ingrained in pubs all over the country. And even though we sort of know that it's a marketing ploy and that the drink wouldn't taste different in the wrong glass, we still want it in the right glass. I'm okay with that. It's polite! It's civilised!

You only have to look at the phenomenon of the Shit London Guinness Instagram account (see also pages 16–18) to understand how easily outraged a pint lover can get about drinks served in the wrong glass. Pictures of badly poured Guinness with no head or some with half a glass of head. Those are upsetting enough but what really gets people (including me) riled up is Guinness in the wrong glass. There are pints in stemmed San Miguel and Stella glasses, in tall Asahi glasses and Foster's glasses! But the worst I've ever seen is Guinness in a glass boot.

Stolen pint glasses

We've all got a pint glass (or three) at home. But where did they come from? Stolen, most likely. But we don't think of it like that. There are people I know who would never dream of shoplifting or stealing who have stolen pub pint glasses in their press at home.

Whether you steal it on purpose or not, it's a rite of passage. Sometimes you don't even realise you're doing it. It's closing time but you haven't finished your pint, so you're going to finish it outside. It feels irresponsible to leave it on the street so the only polite thing to do is to bring it home.

Sometimes you just like the look of a pint glass and you take it home. Sometimes you convince yourself it's a Robin Hood situation, like when you were a student and you genuinely didn't have any glasses in your gaff so you stole out of necessity. There is a widespread belief that the breweries give the pubs the glasses for free, so why not take them home? Will anyone really miss them?

Taking home a pint glass may seem like drunk reasoning, but where does it stop? When ashtrays were a thing, they were put in bags too. I'm sure many other knick-knacks have made their way home. Bar stools are even thought of as fair game too.

My local in London for a long time was the Cow in Westbourne Grove. It was more an Irish-leaning pub than your typical 'Oirish' pub in London. The best seats in the house were the two bar stools at the net curtained window. And the bar stools? They were shaped like pints of Guinness. I remember a scandal sometime in the 2000s when someone managed to rob one of these giant Guinness stools from the pub. I don't recall how it happened or if it was ever returned. It was before such things were shared on social media so I only have my own memory of this to go on, although I do know those bar stools haven't been in the Cow for a long time.

In Dublin more recently, the Black Wolf in Blanchardstown took to Facebook on 30 October 2019 to tell the story of their stolen bar stools. 'People do silly things when they are drunk,' they said, then went on to share the apology letter that was handed back with the bar stools that 'magically reappeared'. The apology read:

> My 31-year-old father-of-two friend thought he was a gas man running out with a barstool in hand on Sunday night. His 31-year-old (SIC) thought it was even funnier taking a second one! Well, I'm left to return them. They're lovely stools, they just don't go with my kitchen! Sorry!

The pub certainly saw the funny side, laughing at the idea of 'the two lads bailing out with a stool in hand running down the road thinking they have pulled off the crime of the century!'

Taking a pint glass pales in comparison.

SECRET CODES ON PINT GLASSES

Now it's time to dig out that glass you stole and check how old it is. Did you know the digits beside the M refer to the year it was made? According to the National Standard Authority of Ireland:

> A pint glass (capacity serving measure) in Ireland should have the following markings to comply with the measuring instruments directive under SI No. 2 of 2018.
>
> A. CE marking and Supplementary Metrology marking (M) and the last two digits of the year of its affixing surrounded by a rectangle which indicates that the instrument complies with the regulation
> B. Number of the notified body who performed the conformity assessment – e.g., '0709'
> C. Measuring capacity – for e.g., 'Pint' that indicates the capacity of the instrument

PINTS, PUBS AND POETS

There is an unwritten rule in Ireland that going for a pint – in particular, stout – in a certain type of pub is considered a more civilised act than, say, going for a vodka and Coke in a club or student bar or anywhere that isn't a proper pub. Certain pints have a superior reputation over other drinks, which on the one hand is ridiculous because a drink is a drink, you would think. But not in Ireland, and not when it comes to the pint. The pint, in particular stout, is often put on a pedestal and I think a huge part of that is thanks to its cosy relationship with Irish literature. Rubbing shoulders with poets and playwrights pays off.

Ireland has a proud literary reputation. We boast a long history of producing some of the world's most celebrated writers. Joyce, Wilde, Yeats, Beckett, Swift – famous names that affirm we are an island of storytellers. They are also famous names that the pint loves to be associated with. Dublin in particular harnesses this well. Many of the best-known writers are seen as part of Dublin's DNA, so it's no surprise that they have a place in pub and pint culture too. The city streets swarm with past literary lives. The pub and the pen go hand in hand.

It helps that many of the pubs still look and feel the way we imagine they did when Oscar Wilde or Brendan Behan sat there contemplating their next words. Many pubs still have seats and snugs preserved as they were. There are gallery walls and murals of our famous writers inside and outside, announcing them as literary pubs. You can go on a literary pub crawl. You can visit pubs mentioned in books and plays or have a pint in pubs named after writers and their works. It's not hard to find the ghosts of writers past when you go for a pint in Dublin.

There are many claims as to where the Dublin literati drank. I'm not going to delve into them all here – plenty of books have been written on the subject and pub crawls that can inform you better – but here are a few of the associations that have done wonders for the reputation of the pint in some manner, starting with James Joyce.

James Joyce

Joyce wrote so much about Dublin that he once claimed if Dublin ever disappeared, you could rebuild it through his words. Even if, like most of us, you've never read *Ulysses*, you probably know about Leopold Bloom, Joyce's fictional protagonist and hero, who said, 'Good puzzle would be to cross Dublin without passing a pub.'

Davy Byrnes In *Ulysses* Bloom visits many pubs, most famously Davy Byrnes on Duke Street, where he orders a glass of Burgundy and a Gorgonzola sandwich.

....

Barney Kiernan's Pints are brilliantly referred to as 'wine of the country' in the 'Cyclops' episode of *Ulysses*.

In 1982, Joyce's centenary, Guinness, ever the astute marketers, printed an ad in the *Irish Times* that claimed, 'When it came to writing slogans James Joyce proved himself no slouch. He suggested replacing 'Guinness is Good for You' with 'Guinness – The Free, The Flow, The Frothy Freshener!' It's a great story but it turns out there is no evidence in the Guinness archive collection that this slogan was ever actually submitted to the brewery by Joyce and it was never used by Guinness on any official advertising. Despite this, it has often been repeated, including on that 1982 centenary advert.

Bloom is in Barney Kiernan's pub (which is no longer around) and Joe Hynes is buying a round:

> **❝** I've a thirst on me I wouldn't sell for half a crown.
>
> Give it a name, citizen, says Joe.
>
> Wine of the country, says he.
>
> What's yours? says Joe.
>
> Ditto MacAnaspey, says I.
>
> Three pints, Terry, says Joe. And how's the old heart, citizen? says he.

....

Mulligan's of Poolbeg Street A pub that sits above them all for Joycean associations has to be Mulligan's of Poolbeg Street because it's alleged this was where Joyce himself drank. He also features it in his story 'Counterparts' in *Dubliners*. When John F. Kennedy visited Dublin it's said that he went to Mulligan's just so he could sit on the same stool that Joyce had.

....

Other notable *Ulysses* mentions J. & M. Cleary's on Amiens Street is better known for its associations with Michael Collins but it's also mentioned in *Ulysses* under its old trading name, the Signal House.

The International Bar on Wicklow Street was known as Ruggy O'Donohoe's in *Ulysses*.

The Oval Bar on Middle Abbey Street, mentioned in the 'Aeolus' chapter, is still going strong.

Conway's on Westland Row, known today as Kennedy's, is still a great spot for a pint.

....

Dublin pubs the literati drank in

The Bailey Formerly called the Maltings, this pub has many literary connections listed on its website, including Evelyn Waugh, John Betjeman, Oliver St John Gogarty and Padraic Colum. It also says that during the 1950s and 60s, publican John Ryan 'maintained close relationships with all of the significant figures of this period, such as Patrick Kavanagh, Samuel Beckett, Brendan Behan, Brian O'Nolan [aka Flann O'Brien] and J.P. Donleavy, many of whom he also supported financially'.

....

The Brazen Head This pub dates back to 1198 and is said to have been Jonathan Swift's local.

....

The Duke Its website highlights the Duke's 'distinguished association with Ireland's literary greats', including James Stephens, James Joyce, Oliver St John Gogarty and Arthur Griffith, who 'breezed into the Duke regularly in the early days of the century when they wanted a quiet reflective jar':

❝ In later years, the three great literary musketeers, Brendan Behan, Patrick Kavanagh and Myles Na gCopoleen, experienced a transitory love affair with the premises, although hardly ever at the same time as they were rarely enamoured with each other's company for too long. As a general rule, the presence of one was dictated by the absence of the other two.

....

Kennedy's According to their website, Kennedy's 'enjoyed the custom of both Beckett and Joyce during their formative years'. When the pub was a grocery shop, it's where 'Oscar Wilde earned his first shilling stacking the shelves on Saturday afternoon'.

....

McDaid's and Grogan's How these two pubs are intertwined is as good a story as any that the literati could have written. Let's start with what exactly constitutes a true literary pub. In *Dublin Pub Life and Lore*, Kevin C. Kearns writes:

> In general terms it has come to mean a public house where a significant number of known writers and intellectuals congregate on a regular basis to discuss matters of literature as well as every other subject under the sun. Over the centuries certain pubs served as gathering places for Dublin's novelists, poets and journalists who found the social environment fertile ground for observing the human condition and exchanging thoughts and ideas. Historically, a number of Dublin pubs took on a literary patronage and ambience as a result of their proximity to bookshops and publishers' offices.

One such pub was McDaid's on Harry Street, just off Grafton Street in Dublin's city centre. Kearns writes that at one time, McDaid's was the archetypal Dublin literary pub:

> In its halcyon days of the 1940s and 1950s McDaid's boasted the grandest galaxy of literary luminaries on the Dublin scene. Regulars included Brendan Behan, Patrick Kavanagh, Brian O'Nolan, Gainor Crist, Austin Clarke, Anthony Cronin, Brian Donleavy, Liam O'Flaherty and others – the collective likes of which Dublin will likely never again see within the walls of one pub.

A big part of the appeal was said to be Paddy O'Brien, the head barman at McDaid's for nearly 35 years, who's been called one of the greatest barmen of all time. And for good reason.

It had been Paddy O'Brien's dream to own his own pub, so when McDaid's was put up for sale in 1972 he went for it, only to be outbid by a wealthy woman from London who wanted to own a literary pub. Coincidentally, at the same time a friend of O'Brien's, Tommy Smith, had just purchased a pub around the corner, the Castle Lounge, better known these days as Grogan's. O'Brien was offered the role of manager. He accepted and it changed the course of literary pub history, as outlined by Donal Fallon in his book *Three Castles Burning*:

> Scooping O'Brien from McDaid's had ensured a readymade clientele that would migrate from one public house to the other. Tommy, capturing the changing city, recalled how 'they just walked across the former car park where the Westbury Hotel now stands'. In the words of the artist Robert Ballagh, who delivered Tommy's funeral oration, it was akin to 'seagulls following a trawler'.

....

Mulligan's of Poolbeg Street We've already pointed out Joyce's preference for this pub but it also lays claim to being a usual stop for Brendan Behan.

....

Neary's Another favourite of Brendan Behan dates back to 1887. Its closeness to the Gaiety Theatre means it's no doubt held court for many a thespian over the years too. The greatest story to come from a writer's visit here, though, has to be that of acclaimed journalist and playwright Nell McCafferty – see 'Women, pubs and pints'.

....

The Palace This pub was a favourite for many writers because of its proximity to the *Irish Times* offices. Writers would hope to curry favour with editors there and journalists would drink there. Those writers included 'the three literary musketeers, Kavanagh, Behan and Myles', who, according to the Palace website, 'shared a great affinity with alcohol, and in particular the Palace Bar, though not necessarily in one another's company'.

....

Searson's Patrick Kavanagh lived on nearby Pembroke Street, and according to the Searson's website he would pass the pub with gusto en route to the city centre to sell his works. On the days it all worked out, 'Kavanagh danced with delight all the way back to Baggot St. when successful, where he gleefully drank half his earnings in Searson's.'

....

Toners Did W.B. Yeats drink in Toners? I've come across varying accounts. Some say Toners was the only pub W.B. Yeats would have a pint in, implying that he drank there a good bit. But another story alleges that he only ever entered the pub once with the poet Oliver St John Gogarty. Apparently they visited the snug but Yeats was so unimpressed that he never set foot in a pub again. I've no idea which story is correct. As Yeats himself said, 'What can be explained is not poetry.'

Toners does have some more solid associations with James Joyce and Patrick Kavanagh, though, who were regulars – so much so that they are depicted on the sign hanging from the pub on Baggot Street.

....

Was Flann O'Brien the OG Guinness influencer? In the poem 'The Workman's Friend' by Brian O'Nolan (better known by his pen name Flann O'Brien), he immortalises the phrase 'a pint of plain is your only man'. The poem implies rather handily that a pint of stout might just solve all your problems.

....

PRICE OF PINTS

Nowhere on the planet do people obsess about the price of a pint like we do in Ireland.

Price changes in the pint in Ireland result in national headlines like 'Beer we go again', 'Rip-Off Republic' and 'It's UnBEERlievable' as outraged journalists and pint drinkers lament the state of the country based on the latest price hike.

Over the last few years, social media has been awash with pictures of people's receipts naming and shaming pubs that dare to charge more than the basic minimum for a pint. 'It's a disgrace!' they say. 'What's the country coming to?' There was much furore recently when it was reported far and wide that a Temple Bar pub was charging €10.45 for a pint of cider. The source of the story? A receipt shared on social media.

It's nothing new. We've been obsessed with the price of our drink ever since it was first taxed in Ireland in 1188, although in the early days, when beer was an essential part of our diet, it was about keeping the price low. Those were the days.

Writing about beer pricing in his book *The Story of the Irish Pub*, Cian Molloy says that in 1256, 'Henry III fixed the price of two basic foodstuffs: bread and beer. Any baker found guilty of overcharging was put in stocks and pilloried, but the penalty for brewers and alehouse keepers who overcharged was a potentially fatal punishment by ducking stool.'

By the late 1800s, price wars were already starting to happen. Molloy writes that from 1862, when Guinness broke an agreement that Dublin brewers had made about discounting, 'the brewery waged a price war that saw its profit margins decrease by 30% while its market share continued to increase. Gradually, Guinness's rivals merged, went out of business or were bought up by the now giant Dublin brewery.'

This is in stark contrast to recent pint price fluctuations, where Guinness (Diageo) has hiked up the price of their pint to much indignation from the trade and customers alike. We've been at it for generations – governments facing off with publicans, drink manufacturers and the public as they attempt to walk the fine line between order and all-out mutiny. There have been Guinness boycotts, High Court challenges, state-imposed price freezes and pickets outside pubs. Every price rise is dubbed the 'nail in the coffin' for pints. Yet here we are, reluctantly paying more than ever, grumbling just as much as we did 50 years ago when customers in one Wicklow pub walked out over a 2p price hike.

PUB CRAWLS

While some people love the idea of walking around in a gang from pub to pub, for others this feels silly, like you're wearing a sign that says, We are tourists! However, I've learned from partaking in a few pub crawls that the fun far outweighs the initial embarrassment (mostly).

A pub crawl with a bit of culture
An excellent example is the famous literary pub crawl in Dublin. This is all about soaking up the culture and learning a few titbits of info you can use to show off to your friends while engaging in a few tasty scoops.

A pub crawl with no culture
This pub crawl is not about the pints or the pubs. This is about backpackers meeting new drinking buddies and the main aim is to get boozy. There will be an overly enthusiastic guide, shots and games. Not for the faint-hearted.

A semi-organised or self-guided pub crawl
This encapsulates the majority of pub crawls we end up on. It could be a birthday pub crawl, a hen party or a stag do, the 12 pubs of Christmas (see also page 60) or perhaps you're just away for the weekend in a town that is crying out to be pub crawled around. While great in theory, these pub crawls are highly subjective and can end up being the best or the worst day or night of your life.

The accidental pub crawl
You don't even realise you're on it until pub number three. Everything has just come together well and the pints are flowing. Perfect.

QUIET PINTS

The quiet pint is a thing of beauty. Ideally, it's taken solo. You head to the pub on your own and order a pint. You might sit at the bar or nab a table to yourself. You've no agenda. You're not waiting for anyone. You sip your pint and contemplate whatever is on your mind. Maybe you bring a book along, maybe the paper; perhaps you do a crossword. You might have a brief chat with the bar staff or nod at a few other punters, but the important bit here is that you are on your own, enjoying your quiet pint.

This is another pint moment that has been quite romanticised. It was certainly a romantic pint dream of mine early on. I did it for the first time when I was 18 or 19. I'd moved out of my family home into a dingy ground-floor flat in a Victorian redbrick in Portobello, Dublin. I figured if I could pay my own rent (just about), surely I could go out for a pint alone, so I did. I chose the Bleeding Horse at the top of Camden Street because it seemed like an approachable pub where I wouldn't stick out too much. I brought the *Irish Times* with me, crossword at the ready (Simplex), ordered a Guinness and settled in. I felt so grown up. I boasted about it later to some friends. The boys didn't seem too impressed – I guess they didn't realise it was a big deal. The girls thought I was mad or that I was out trying to get chatted up.

You see, even though enjoying a quiet pint is a wonderful experience, it's not the same experience for everyone. There is a type we think of when drinking a pint alone: males, usually over a certain age. They approach the solo pint with ease, like they were born to do it. They probably don't think twice or have to worry about being stared at, questioned or approached

WORDLE

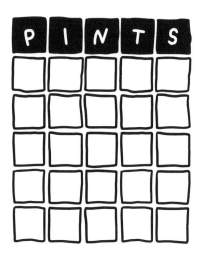

— an unfortunate blight for women or anyone who might not fit the typical solo pint drinker bill doing the same thing. But please, don't let that put you off.

I contemplated writing a few pointers here on how to make going for a solo pint more approachable and pleasant if you aren't the stereotypical solo pint drinker but fuck that. Everyone should be a solo drinker. Just give it a try. Pick a pub you like. Sure, it helps to bring along a book or a paper or do your Wordle, but do whatever you want. If you get strange looks, give them a wave. If you get unwanted attention, tell them it's unwanted. Do whatever you can to make sure your quiet pint is just as you intended it to be: quiet.

ROUNDS

When you drink pints in Ireland, at some stage you're going to end up in a round.

This is not something to be taken lightly. Irish rounds are a particular thing, a ritual intrinsically linked to our drinking and pub culture. There are rules, peculiarities and complexities akin to being in a secret society.

Rounds can appear to be an exceptionally simple concept. You take turns buying drinks – easy-peasy. But drinkers beware. If you get it wrong, it can ruin your reputation, sully or even end friendships. You do not want to be known as the one who never gets their round in. Being thought of as cheap in Ireland is one of our biggest fears, ingrained into us since the days of Brehon Law (see also 'Pints: An origin story'). Generosity was, and still is, something we want to embody, hence the fear when it comes to getting things wrong in a round.

It should be smooth and straightforward, an act of common courtesy, but it's also based on trust and fairness. And when there's drink involved, that can be tricky. So a few rules are needed to make it work. A plethora of mostly unspoken rules that should be adhered to. An etiquette, certain implications and of course exceptions. Oh, and an assumption of knowledge of all these.

So you see, it's not so simple. But once you get to grips with it, it's a bit like riding a bike: once you know, you know forever.

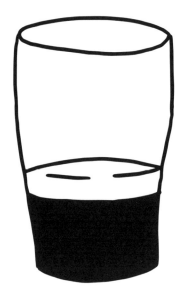

ANOTHER?

> ❝ The Irish don't go in for the Dutch treat system. If five men enter a pub, each will stand a round, and etiquette demands that all stay until the last of the five rounds has been bought. If you are invited to join such a group, and do so, remember that you will give offense by a refusal to treat and be treated... **A Pocket Guide to Northern Ireland, issued by Special Service Division, United States Army, 1942**

The basic rules of rounds

The old rules of rounds dictated that we keep going till the other person stops, drops or it's closing time. These days, we are generally more responsible. Stop when you want! But there are still rules to be followed.

- When two or more people are in a pub together, assume you are going to be doing rounds. This is when one person buys a 'round' of drinks for the whole group.
- It's not an act of generosity – it's a system. The expectation is that if you've been bought a drink in a round, you will take a turn to buy a round. Each person in the group has a turn, then it starts again with the first buyer.
- Buying the round means you are also responsible for taking the order and going to the bar, bringing back the drinks and making sure everyone has what they need.

Rounds these days are more accepting, but there is still a certain etiquette to consider.

Timing the rounds

- You should never, ever let the pints go fully empty before you order the next round, especially when drinking stout. The acceptable time to initiate the next round is generally when about one-third of the drink is left in the glass. If it's your round, then it's time to act. If it's not your round and you're drinking faster than the person whose round it is, it's polite to linger and slow down at this point.

- If the person whose round it is doesn't seem to be taking the initiative, you can subtly (or not!) let them know where you are in your pint by taking your next sip with an exaggerated *mmm* or *ahhh* as you place your glass down, pretending you're savouring it or signalling its deliciousness, but really you're saying, 'Hey, buddy, it's your round.'

Round exceptions and evaders

- There is an expectation that you know the price of your drink. If you're a top-shelf whiskey drinker or knocking back premium spirits and mixers, rounds are generally not the place for these – unless, of course, the person you're with is drinking the same thing. You need to read the room. If your gin and tonic is twice the price of the pints everyone else is drinking, this is not polite round etiquette. You could lower your standards and drink the house gin and plain mixer or you can acknowledge that you're being boujee and will break out on your own. Often there could be someone in the group longing for a fishbowl full of expensive gin instead of a pint of plain and they may offer themselves up to 'go in with you'. It's a win-win and no one goes home giving out about the drinks you ordered.

- There are, of course, times you go to the pub and are genuinely only staying for one. You should let this be known up top and it's fine to just get your own drink, separate from the round. Someone may unwittingly include you in the first round before you get to do this. If that happens, you will be expected to let them know – more than once – that you will get them back next time.

- Anyone not drinking alcohol but still ordering a drink should usually be included in the round but they are not expected to get a round in if they are only on water or a soft drink. If they are drinking something non-alcoholic that has a similar monetary value to the pint, then they are in the round. This also depends on the size of the group. There was a time in Ireland when not drinking was a reason for slagging someone but these days most people have the cop-on to just shut up and do their own thing – as they should.

Even more notes on rounds
- Volunteer for your round early on. You'll be in good favour if you buy your round while everyone still remembers.
- If you are the host or the arranger of the meet-up, you should buy the first round.
- If it's your birthday, wedding, etc. you may be told not to buy a round (but you still probably should).
- The person who makes the biggest deal of getting the round is the person watching to see if everyone buys their round.
- Someone should be vaguely keeping track but you don't want to look like the person who's keeping track. It's a complex game.
- Don't expect it to be even-stevens in every session. There is usually someone more eager/thirsty/cash rich who will buy more out of turn, and there may also be someone who's avoiding their round. Depending on how well you know the gang you are with, you can speak up but usually you just nod and keep drinking.
- Buying crisps when it's your round is never a bad idea.
- If all else fails, put your faith in drink karma, a concept that Judith Boyle, beer sommelier and publican, shared with me when we spoke about our fear of rounds. Her philosophy is to always get a round in early and don't worry too much about getting your drink back that session because: drink karma! 'You meet people and you buy them a drink. They're like, "Oh, I'll get you back," but I say, "No, it's drink karma." Your drink will always come back to you in Ireland.'

THE SESH

According to the *Oxford English Dictionary*, the sesh is:

Sesh: A *session or bout, esp. of drinking.*

A sesh, as the dictionary says, is a bout of drinking, but it's also so much more than that. Just as pints have a separate universe in Ireland, so, too, does the sesh. Even uttering the words can induce the fear (see page 102) if you've been on a big sesh recently or pure giddiness if you're due a sesh.

There are many layers to a sesh. It's often in multiple locations, a cousin of the pub crawl. It can grow, expand, shrink and grow again, all in one night. People dip in and out. Texts are sent. More people join. There are trips to the shops for the smokers. Crisps are probably eaten for dinner (see also 'Crisps and pints').

You might have cut your teeth on the sesh when you were a student. It suits a lifestyle where you can slack off the next day if needs be without major consequences. An article by Bridget Maloney in *Trinity News* in September 2018, 'An ode to the sesh', tells us of the importance of the sesh to university students: 'The "sesh", as we call it today, has been the cornerstone of Irish student culture for centuries.' She goes on:

❝ The 'sesh', in all of its forms, endures to this day as the main social outlet for Irish university students. It is a way to momentarily put aside the academic strains of university and enjoy the social side that college has to offer. In celebration or in despair, the versatility of the ritual is what makes it so omnipresent in our country. The 'sesh' is a truly time-honoured tradition that has existed nearly as long as Ireland itself, making it an integral part of the culture and embedding it into our national character.

There's usually a lot of alcohol consumed but it's not just about the booze, especially (and ironically) if you're in a pub. Although the sesh might start in a pub, it can end anywhere. An unplanned sesh is always far superior to the planned ones but both are a lot of fun and anything can happen. Andrea Horan, cultural commentator and founder of Tropical Popical in Dublin, has spoken many times about 'the power of the sesh', particularly when it ends up on the dance floor. I asked her what makes it so special:

❝ Magical things happen on a dance floor.

And afterwards. People are joined in unity, from a broad spectrum of society, and disagreements about politics and policies are forgotten as people are all brought together with common purpose in unified movement and energy.

Apart from the joy that is created – and surely the creation of joy should be enough to justify or validate any experience, for what other purpose is there to life than communal and shared joy? – many social movements have begun through shared experiences and conversations that go on late in the night and early into the morning. The world has been changed by conversations that started on a dance floor.

She's not wrong. When pints evolve to a sesh, anything can happen. It can be a way to bond like no other, to make friends and more. To make connections, even network sometimes. And it's nothing new. Andrea continues:

" Every historical record we have was about people coming together to celebrate at festivals – to mark harvests, seasons, events and life events. The ritual of celebration gives our lives meaning. It brings us together and helps us to overcome adversity. And most importantly, it's fun. Is that not enough?

During the covid lockdowns in 2020 and 2021, when Ireland missed the sesh, entrepreneur and social media star James Kavanagh launched a streetwear brand on the back of how much we wanted the sesh back in our lives. He designed clothing and totes with the words *Tíocfaidh ár Sesh* emblazoned across them, disco ball and all. 'We'll kiss, dance and laugh again soon. Our sesh will come' was the motto. The proceeds went to Inner City Helping Homeless and the National Campaign for the Arts.

SILVER SCREEN PINTS

We see a lot of booze on the silver screen. It's a constant hack for storytelling, fuelling the brave and adding to the drama. But it's rare to see pints in among the action. Not in Hollywood, anyway. They prefer moody glasses of scotch and glistening ice-cold martinis for seminal moments.

Even in TV shows, I struggle to think of pints being showcased the way cocktails have. Cocktails have a great time! Sometimes they could even be considered a supporting actor. Think of the cosmopolitans on *Sex and the City* or Don Draper's old-fashioned on *Mad Men*. When we do see beers and pints on screen, they say everyday, working class – think *Corrie*, *Eastenders* and *Cheers*.

American TV and movies have a particular type of beer-drinking moment. Beer is used in scenes when a director wants to indicate that two characters are bonding. Think of a detective show when the two battling partners share a beer and discover what they have in common. Beer together = best buds. Troublesome dialogue? Bring in the beers. Want the audience to see a character as 'one of us'? Give them a beer. How many times have you seen lawyers clinking bottles of beer after a long day in court, jocks pouring kegs into red cups at frat parties, or buddy and hang-out movies that centre around beer? Beers and more beers. But it's still not *pints*.

The pints we know and love? There aren't enough of them. Even when we do see them on screen, they suffer from terrible stereotyping. First it's probably going to be a man you see drinking a pint. Second, he's probably not the swashbuckling hero type, but an everyday man, a working-class man or sometimes the shouldn't-you-be-doing-something-other-than-drinking man.

Worse than that are the old-school American movies made in Ireland where they like to depict pub patrons as simplistic and gullible. In his book *Have Ye No Homes to Go To?*, Kevin Martin mentions the 1970s movie *Quackser Fortune Has a Cousin in the Bronx* and writes, 'The lack of intellectual ability is a theme running through representations of the Irish pub in American-made films.' He also references the 1959 movie *Darby O'Gill and the Little People* featuring Sean Connery and the worst Irish accent of all time. In the fictional local pub, the Rathmullen Arms, the patrons are depicted as 'wide-eyed simpletons who gape in wonder'.

It's a trope that's still hanging around. In the 2010 movie *Leap Year* starring Amy Adams, she arrives in Ireland by boat and gets stranded. She heads to a rural pub for help, where the dumbed-down locals stare in awe like they've never seen a woman before. It's supposed to be set around the time it was filmed, in 2010. Her next stop is a pub called Big Tom, where the locals usurp her suitcase and put her bras on their heads. It ends in a brawl. Perhaps there's a saving grace in that the pints at least look good (interestingly, in real life Amy Adams is a fan of pints of Guinness).

Two of the best-known American-made Irish movies, *The Quiet Man* and *Ryan's Daughter*, both have seminal scenes in pubs. Some depict a bit more conviviality but there are also dark, dramatic moments to be had.

There are exceptions, of course, when the pub is captured as we know it. There are epic pint-drinking moments on screen, just not enough of them. This is my call for some more. Give pints the pedestal they deserve!

O'SCAR

Here are four famous pints and pubs on screen worth a mention. (Warning: There are spoilers!)

The Snapper

This iconic Irish film is based on a novel by Roddy Doyle and directed by Stephen Frears. They both clearly understand the role a pint plays in many Irish lives and capture it superbly on screen from the first pub scene where Sharon Curley (Tina Kellegher) tells her dad, Dessie Curley (Colm Meaney), that she's expecting a little 'snapper'. Meaney takes a gulp of his pint, too shocked to wipe off his Guinness moustache as the news is delivered. Most of Meaney's scenes outside the home are in the pub, talking with his cronies over perfect-looking pints in no-nonsense tulip glasses. The finest moment for the pint, though, is the end scene when the baby has arrived safe and sound weighing a healthy seven pounds twelve ounces:

One of Dessie Curley's drinking buddies who tries to help him through his difficult time by drinking pints is Lester, played by Brendan Gleeson, who has more recently and more famously sipped pints on screen with Colin Farrell.

❝ Seven pounds twelve ounces, wha?'

'Is that a turkey or a baby?'

'It's a baby!'

'That's a good-sized baby.'

'It is, bud, isn't it?'

'Small turkey, though.'

We see the family celebrate, then it cuts back to Dessie, who finishes his pint in one go. After months of not being able to enjoy his pint, is this our signal that he's accepted the 'snapper' now?

The Banshees of Inisherin

Much of the drama in this hugely successful Irish film – including Brendan Gleeson's now-iconic 'I just don't like you no more' line – happens in the fictional J.J. Devine's pub as the lads sup on a pair of pints. But it was a travesty for the pint to make it to the Oscars and then be depicted as a crutch for a crumbling, angst-ridden, spiteful relationship, never mind the fact that the pints themselves didn't look great. I suppose we hoped for a creamy head, a welcoming pint, the ones we're used to these days, not the drab poured-from-a-bottle type the whole world saw on screen. To be fair, though, this is how it was most likely served in the 1920s, when the film is set. I can, however, confirm that the real-life modern-day pints served on Achill Island and Inis Mor are much, much better.

Apparently they used non-alcoholic Guinness 0.0 on set, which the actors praised as an excellent alternative to the concoctions they've been presented with on set before, which include drinking grape juice with cream. Ugh.

P.S. I Love You

You weren't expecting that one, were you? This movie is based on a novel by Celia Ahern and tells the story of Holly Kennedy's (Hilary Swank) grief for her dead husband, Gerry (Gerald Butler). But there is some other grief featured here: grief for the undrunk pints!

When Holly visits Ireland, she has the *grá* for the Guinness. We see her with a lovely pint in a snug in her dead husband's favourite pub (filmed in Whelan's) as she plucks up the courage to talk to William (Jeffrey Dean Morgan). He's just finished singing on stage and is also sipping on a

Guinness. Holly forgoes her creamy specimen to chat him up as we see the pint darken in the distance. There's hope a few minutes later as she's bopping along to a flashback of her dead husband singing 'Galway Girl' while she drinks another pint. The head looks a bit big on this one, but it's a gig pint so it's forgivable. Alas, she ends up giving away the pint because William's leaning in for the shift (at least that bit is understandable).

Despite Holly's reluctance to drink the actual pints, this movie gets a mention because these are the pints I want to see more of on screen. They are not scene stealers, but rather scene setters. Romantic comedies based in Ireland tend to favour the twee, creating scenes we would never really do here (see *Leap Year!*). This scene? It just looks right. Despite the rest of the Irishness of the film feeling hammy in parts, this scene does not – and I credit the pints with that.

Dublin Oldschool

This Irish movie about a wannabe DJ, Jason, as he stumbles from one session to the next is definitely more drug than booze fuelled but there are a couple of pint moments that deserve a mention because they are pretty spot on.

Early in Jason's adventure, he makes a pit spot at Dublin pub institution Grogan's with his pal who tells him, 'Settle, petal, I'll get ya a nice little pint.' The lads look shifty and drink lager while the locals around them sip good-looking pints of the black stuff.

The next day there's a scene where the pals are on the rollover pints before they head to the next session. It's in Anseo on Camden Street. As soon as anyone joins them to sit, someone says, 'Pint?' It captures that lazy, hungover vibe perfectly, with drinks going down slowly and people wearing sunglasses inside, hoping that the hangover will be fixed by the next pint (see also 'Hangover pints').

SLÁINTE

Sláinte is probably the best-known Irish phrase around the world and it's often said with a pint in hand. The direct translation means 'health' but we use it as a cheers, so we are really saying, 'To your health!'

You love to see *cúpla focail* (a few words) of Gaeilge (Irish) being said casually. Every little helps when it comes to keeping the language alive. Gaeilge is the first official language of Ireland, having been spoken for thousands of years, right up until the British invasion and 800-year-plus rule over Ireland. Oppressive laws and Irish being outlawed in schools meant our native language diminished as our spoken tongue. These days, even though most of us still learn Irish in school, it's not widely spoken and remains the daily language in only some areas of the country called the Gaeltacht.

When you're headed to the *leithras* (bathroom) it's important to know that *mná* = women and *fir* = men.

This means any Irish being spoken, even just the odd *sláinte*, matters. So next time you're going for a *pointa* (pint), why not try to add in a few more *focail as Gaeilge* yourself?

SNUGS

Finding a great pub that pours great pints is a perfect moment in and of itself. But if that great pub has a snug and you get a seat in said snug? There's nothing better.

'In the snug' is the text you long to get when heading to meet a friend for a pint. Closed-off, private rooms steeped in history. Wood panelling. Probably some frosted or stained glass. An ancient door. A hatch to order your drinks directly from the bar. The seats are usually wooden benches and are never comfy, but who cares? You're in the snug! Tucked-away corners you can settle into – and you must settle in, because if you've got that coveted seat, you hang on to it. It's a reason to cancel dinner plans and stay put.

But beware! You can be guaranteed there's someone else in that pub watching your every move to see if you'll be leaving anytime soon. Watch out for these snug cuckoos. They'll flit around looking for a moment of weakness. Maybe there are only two of you in there. 'Oh, can I join you?' they say, but then their friends start to arrive in. How do I know? Because I am that snug cuckoo. I can't help it. I'm drawn to the snug. If there's one in the pub, I want to be in it. I want to settle in there. I want to pint there.

The irony of the origin of the snug is not lost on me every time I go out of my way to secure a spot in one. For a long time, the snug was the only place women might be allowed to have a drink – if they were allowed in the pub at all, that is (see also 'Women, pubs and pints').

I'M OFF TO THE SNUG

Snugs originally appeared in Ireland in the 19th century. There was a push to make the beautiful Victorian pubs more respectable, so snugs were built in or added. They are usually wooden compartments on the side of the bar offering a cloak of privacy and secrecy to those who might not have wanted to be seen in the pub – or those who should not be seen in the pub, such as guards, priests or clergymen, politicians or wealthy patrons who wanted privacy. They might have been used for meetings to buy and sell animals or perhaps a spot of matchmaking. Soldiers might have snuck in for a drink. And of course women. Women were snug regulars.

In the book *Dublin Pub Life and Lore* by Kevin C. Kearns, there is a plethora of snug mentions as his interviewees reminisce about the pubs of Dublin's past. They talk of snugs as 'confession boxes' where 'revered grannies and hardy women street dealers' might meet for 'little sessions'. They'd drink a 'gill' (about a quarter pint) or a 'GP', a glass of plain porter. Ninety-year-old May Hanaphy of the Liberties recalls of the 1920s, 'Oh, a woman'd be murdered if she was caught in a pub.' But Kearns notes:

❝ There were, however, two conspicuous exceptions – revered grannies and hardy women street dealers. Owing to their longevity and difficult life they were excluded from the social mores which barred other women.

They were the ones who might be spotted in a snug with a shawl, sipping a glass of porter and perhaps smoking a clay pipe. The book also has many accounts of snugs being used for political meetings, as they were the perfect places for secret planning.

The storied history of snugs surely only adds to their appeal. It's no wonder we want to sit in them and soak up all that might have happened there before. Here's to that sweet snug life.

SPORTS AND PINTS

You can picture it now: a heaving pub awash with colour, with big screens galore. Pundits bellow down on the masses through speakers as fans queue three deep at the bar. The loos are a no-go zone in the minutes before kick-off/throw-in/whatever you're having yourself. It's noisy. It's packed. Depending on how you feel about the sport or team in question, you're in your rightful place on earth. Or perhaps sport is not your thing, so you turn and leave. Sports in the pub is not for everyone, but for those that it is, it's everything.

Drinking pints while watching sport on the telly is not one size fits all. Some fans are so committed that their drink is secondary. They'll sip it slowly because they're focused so hard on the game, annoyed when people start talking about something other than what's happening on the screen.

Others (me) use whatever happens to be on as an excuse for pints. They'll become more or less invested in the game as the pints go on, depending on how 'we' are doing and how regularly they make it up to the bar.

Then you have the crew who can't pick one over the other, so they commit to them both as if their lives depend on it. C'mon, Ireland! Up the pints!

Sports aren't often mentioned in the many books I've read about the Irish pub and its traditions. It was never really considered a part of the traditional Irish pub, bar a few places that might have a small telly in the corner for horse racing. But in the modern equivalent, sport on TV is like mass was on Sunday. Love it or loathe it, you've been there at some stage.

Occasional sports fans buy into the main events and pubs come alive as the moment approaches. How it pans out varies completely. A cocktail of crushing disappointment with the occasional dash of glory. It's pure sport, in a drinking sense.

It's not just watching on screens, of course. There are the pints that bookend going to an actual match, pints that you might go for after you play a match (see also 'Well-earned pints') and pints that you might drink while you're at a match. Irish people love a team sport. We love watching matches, supporting teams, wearing team colours and getting together to roar at pitches or screens – often with a pint in hand.

World Cup matches, in particular Italia '90

Italia '90 marked an Irish coming of age. It was our first time on the world stage, and we liked it. I remember being swept up in the occasion, like millions of others. Thousands of Irish begged, borrowed and stole to travel to Italy for the World Cup, but as the great writer Con Houlihan later quipped, 'Italia '90? I missed it … I was in Italy at the time.'

The *Evening Press* stalwart rued missing out on the mother and father of all parties back home when everyone went football mad as Jack Charlton's lads reached the quarter-finals.

RTÉ and other media broadcast and reported from pubs, where the public lost their collective minds over several hours of poor enough quality football. You could watch the match at home, of course, but watching a match in the pub, for something that big, is a particular thing. The *craic*, the camaraderie, the elation.

Roddy Doyle captures it well in his book *The Van*, which is set against the background of Italia '90:

❝ The place went fuckin' mad!

Ireland had got the equaliser.

Jimmy Sr grabbed Bimbo and nearly broke him in half with the hug he gave him. Bertie was up on one of the tables thumping his chest. Even Paddy, the crankiest fucker ever invented, was jumping up and down and shaking his arse like a Brazilian. All sorts of glasses toppled off the tables but no one gave a fuck. Ireland had scored against England and there was nothing more important than that, not even your pint.

Who scored it!? Who scored it? –Don't know. It doesn't fuckin' matter!

Ireland winning any match is a big deal. Getting a result against England on the greatest stage in football? That was unforgettable.

In the film version of *The Van*, pints are flying everywhere in this scene. It's a joy to watch. Or if you really want to relive the moment in a real-life pub, there are videos still floating around online of the RTÉ news segment filmed in Kiely's of Donnybrook (RIP). There's no atmosphere like it.

Italia '90 was also important because it changed the face of who drank in the pub. For the first time, women, kids and everyone else gate-crashed the preserve of the usual suspects.

We've had many World Cups since, of course, a few of which we even reached. A special shout-out for USA 1994, when life was a little more difficult for drinkers as some matches ran into the middle of the night.

Korea/Japan 2002 introduced many fans to the concept of breakfast pints for the first time. Until then, only those acquainted with the infamous early houses (see also pages 71–3) really understood what it was like to down jars that early in the morning. But suddenly, hundreds of thousands of people were faced with the conundrum of the times: push through from the night before or get up and start having pints from 7 a.m.? Many fans were undoubtedly lost to the former, which rarely worked out according to plan.

The Republic of Ireland's women's team's sojourn for the World Cup Down Under in 2023 gave us a taste again of what it was like to have that World Cup buzz. It possibly didn't produce the same levels as Italia '90 but who knows what advancing from the group stages might have fashioned as fans really got into the swing of things? Here's hoping for 2027 – COYGIG!

GAA

GAA (Gaelic Athletic Association) fans are probably the most passionate of all the sports fans in Ireland. It's a club thing or a county thing, but it's where you're from that matters most. We've become much more sophisticated in how the national sports are packaged – the homemade crêpe paper rosettes of the 1980s have made way for slick official merchandise – but the unique privilege of involvement hasn't changed a bit.

Pints play a large part in that. Victory pints, consolation pints, expectancy pints and comeback pints remain at the heart of the supporter experience even as the players move well away from them. And let's not forget the GAA clubhouses, where many a pint has been poured.

Football

Football – or soccer, as some folks call it to differentiate it from Gaelic football – is big business in Ireland, even if a lot of that is exported.

Crowds loyally flock to the Aviva Stadium to watch the Republic of Ireland men's team despite the many disappointments and the burgeoning women's side has been selling out Tallaght Stadium. Tallaght is home to the Shamrock Rovers, who attracted huge crowds in the League of Ireland, a competition growing in stature as clubs all over the country develop strong community roots.

However, our tens of thousands of Premier League tourists spend around £25 million a year following (mostly) Liverpool and Manchester United, but also anyone from Arsenal to Wolves. And when it comes to spending on pints watching these games on the plain old pub TV, we're probably talking GDP-of-small-nations money.

Even as pubs struggle in the face of a health kick revolution and streaming on demand, the big games still pack them out. If Liverpool are in a Champions League final, you'd better make sure you have your table booked or you might not get in.

Following and watching football in Ireland is a national sport in and of itself but we do have an etiquette people must try to abide by.

1   **Except for truly gargantuan occasions, wearing jerseys over the age of 30 if you are watching a match on TV in the pub is frowned upon and rightly so.**
2   **A pub must always indicate whether it operates on a first come, first served basis or is showing the match as advertised. Many an unfortunate party has turned up to watch a game that in their heads was massive, only to find two farmers on an afternoon off watching the racing from Navan. Go on, try to change it to the soccer. I dare you.**
3   **Whether you stand during the national anthem usually depends on how drunk you are, so this can be taken on a case-by-case basis.**

IRFU

I'M REALLY FUCKING UPENDING THESE PINTS

Rugby

Irish rugby has been having quite the moment the last few years. After not being taken seriously outside of the usual pockets for most of the 20th century in Ireland, the last few decades have seen the sport gain huge momentum and a huge following. It's no longer just the preserve of the private schools of the South Dublin suburbs or the working-class areas of Limerick. For many reared hating the sport, watching its renaissance is hard work. Cheering for the goys might not be this lot's cup of tea.

While it's a game for everyone, the South Dublin association will always be there. And let's face it, it's provided much entertainment over the years, particularly from the rugby-obsessed, Heineken-drinking fictional character Ross O'Carroll Kelly (see also page 38). Ross O'Carroll Kelly (ROCK, geddit?) is a creation of writer Paul Howard. Ross epitomises the worst version of an Irish rugby fan, much to Ireland's amusement. Most of the time.

Pints at matches

There is something very Irish about fans of different sports rowing over who gets to bring their pints to their seats during a match and who doesn't. It's also something unique to Ireland that fans are happy enough to risk missing a crucial moment in a game just so they can nip out and get another pint.

Soccer fans attending matches at Ireland's Aviva Stadium are not allowed to bring their pints with them to their seat but rugby fans attending the same venue are allowed. Of course, this stirs up all the usual working class vs. posh class feeling, but it's those killjoys in UEFA who are actually to blame for forcing fans to limit their scoops to halftime, not the FAI. So those supporters who fail to get their smuggled pint in past eagle-eyed security have to down it rapidly behind the stand to make it back in for the second half. Many supporters have it down to a fine art. Sneak out with a few minutes still left on the clock in the first half, order two pints and get them into you over the next 20 minutes. They usually have time to get a quick toilet break in too before getting back in for the second half. Not a moment more than necessary is missed.

The ability of rugby fans to bring their Heinos in with them came under threat in 2022 following a barrage of complaints from supporters fed up with boozehounds flowing in and out at crucial moments to get another drink. Such was the level of discontent that the IRFU seriously considered following the football crowd but they opted to email patrons to request they just show a little decorum instead.

The GAA also insists that their Croke Park public sip their pints before taking their seat or their spot on Hill 16 – although some fans have been known to bend that particular rule. And while we're on the subject of rivalries, stout lovers in Croker sup Guinness, while down in Cork's Páirc Uí Chaoimh, it is of course Murphy's.

I SURVIVED THE PANDEMIC

& ALL I GOT WAS THIS LOUSY PINT

A SUBSTANTIAL
MEAL AND PINTS

After the covid lockdowns in 2020 and 2021, pubs were required to have a food offering in order to reopen and serve pints. It had to be a 'substantial meal' that cost at least €9.00. We were baffled as to how this would protect us from covid but delighted we could go for a pint again, so we headed out and ate overpriced toasties, bad pizzas and everything in between.

The government went back to the Intoxicating Liquor Act of 1962 to define a substantial meal: 'The meal is such as might be expected to be served as a main midday or evening meal or as a main course in either such meal.'

You see, the 'substantial meal' isn't new. It had been a stalwart of a night out in Ireland in the 1980s and 1990s. In order to have a late licence in Ireland, operators were required to include a substantial meal as part of the admission.

I'm of a vintage that I can just about recall this. You could be midway through a slow dance when dinner came out. The music might even stop. Everyone goes to queue up with the raffle ticket they were handed on the way in to exchange it for a chicken curry. You stand around balancing your midnight dinner with your pint. Then before you know it, dinner is done and it's back to the dance floor, belly full.

SUPERPUBS

If you can recall drinking pints of something vaguely European beside a zebra print wall or a Moroccan-inspired tea chest, you'll remember the Irish superpub, an impressive breed of drinking establishment that emerged in the 1990s. The country was changing. We wanted something more than the traditional pub could offer and we found it in superpubs. As these new ventures appeared, we flocked to them. We were young, we were foolish.

In *The Rise and Fall of the Irish Pub*, Robert E. Connolly writes:

> **❛❛** Among the best known successful new age superpubs in Dublin were Café en Seine, Samsara, Ron Blacks (all on Dawson Street), Break for the Border, Zanzibar, Bobs (formerly Bad Bobs), Howl at the Moon, the George and Fireworks. In Galway, the Quays Bar and the Front Door dominated; Cork was represented by Coal Quay and Nancy Spains and Limerick had Flannerys and Nancy Blakes.

A superpub wasn't just a pub that was bigger. It probably had 'trendy décor', most likely a theme. It might serve food, have a dance floor, a DJ booth, maybe a stage or some form of entertainment that didn't just involve being a pub.

> **❛❛** You can be sipping spirits in an African spice island or lowering pints in downtown Moscow. The invasion of the themed super-pubs has received an enthusiastic welcome from all but the most unadventurous socialisers. (***Irish Times*, 1998**)

You could head out early-ish and start on a few pints. There would be cool background music, then as the night wore on, chairs and bar stools disappeared, the lights went down and the music came up or a DJ came on. Before you knew it, you were on the dance floor, drinks sloshing around you. The superpub was far more animated than the usual pub. Before, you might have gone to the pub and then had to find a disco or nightclub after. This gave us a whole night out in one. We were delighted with ourselves.

When it came to pints, all the usual suspects would have been available, of course. No one is going to take that risk. Irish people are mostly creatures of habit when it comes to drinks but for those who wanted to show they were moving with the times, there were new options. Bottles of Grolsch with their quirky flip-top lids, Budvar and pints from Europe we'd never tried before, and of course, sticky cocktails.

They were good times, but they didn't last. By the mid-2000s, the superpub was dwindling. Changing market forces meant the foundations that had led to their development gradually weakened. The smoking ban, the change in drink-driving laws and then of course the recession meant the end of our elaborate drinking dens. The traditional pubs suffered because of these things too, but they (mostly) hadn't ploughed as much investment into ostentatious makeovers as the big superpubs had, although there are certainly places around Ireland where you'll still find a random light-up dance floor or evidence of fish tanks in walls. The hangover from the superpub was a whopper one.

TAKEAWAY PINTS

Up until 2020, plastic pint glasses were what we drank from at festivals (see also 'Festival pints') or in pubs, nightclubs or events that were very busy or tended to get rowdy. They had a time and a place. We put up with them when we had to.

We did not long for them but that all changed in 2020, when the covid pandemic changed our way of life, including our drinking habits. Suddenly a pint in a plastic glass was the ultimate flex. We were seeking them out, queueing for them and, of course, sharing them on social media. We (socially distantly) flocked to them. Some pubs even got inventive and offered delivery. Ice cream vans became pint vans.

The takeaway pint was a saviour. I still remember my first one (or rather, my first four; why would you buy just one?). You had to make sure you were 100m away from the pub before pulling your face mask down for a sip.

Some of us got carried away. Dublin's South William Street in the good weather became party central and caused a bit of a stir. They threatened to take away our takeaway drink privileges but we persevered. We took our pints where we could get them and we cherished them, plastic glasses and all.

TOASTIES AND PINTS

A toastie for dinner is the best friend of the pint. Crisps are great and all, but you're only kidding yourself that it's a dinner (see also 'Crisps and pints'). A toastie (or two), however, can fully be considered a meal – and has been many times for most Irish pint drinkers.

The traditional pub toastie is a particular type of toastie. That's not to say there aren't some wonderful modern iterations available these days using sourdough bread, thick-cut ham and local artisan cheese, etc. They are to be commended and enjoyed. But the stalwart of the pub toastie is the old-school sandwich we know and love that has saved us on many occasions: white sliced pan encasing nondescript cheese and thin slices of deli *hang* (ham).

There are variations on this depending on the pub you're in. Some will have a 'toasted special', which is not a daily special, as the name implies, but a toastie made of ham, cheese, onion and tomato.

Your toastie is usually prepared behind the bar, taken from a fridge stocked with pre-made sandwiches. It's heated between the two hot plates of a sandwich press until the insides are scorching hot. Then it's served with a paper napkin under it, which is more than likely red or burgundy. It's cut into triangles. There's a knife on the side and usually a selection of sachet condiments: mayonnaise, ketchup or mustard if you're feeling sophisticated.

It tastes divine. It hits the spot every time. Mostly because you usually only order it when you've decided to skip dinner and stay in the pub. Just don't forget the all-important pint pairing!

....

Spotted on the Reddit r/ireland forum:

❟❟ One of the chefs in my work just asked why the toasted special is always the same.

'It's so boring. Would it not be better to do a different special each day, like we do with everything else?'

I'm dying here.

....

TOURIST PINTS

Tourist pints encompass quite a few situations, including being a tourist in Ireland, impressing tourists in Ireland or hosting tourists in Ireland. All have one important thing in common: they are all excellent examples of when going for a simple pint is so much more than that.

Being a tourist in Ireland

You're holidaying at home, the weather is going to be unpredictable and it's probably going to cost you four times what it would in a warmer, cheaper part of Europe but you know what you can be guaranteed? A pub. In Ireland, you're never too far from a proper pub and finding a perfect, quintessential old-school pub when you're away is the best (see also 'The old man's pub'). Pubs outside our usual realm of familiarity hold special appeal. You're on holiday so there are no real time restraints. A lunchtime or afternoon pint is often on the cards and they seem even sweeter when you know your colleagues are probably still at work.

You know the pub you're looking for. A quiet spot where locals will turn to look you up and down (see also 'The local'). Inside the décor looks like it's been the same for 50 or maybe even 100 years. There is minimal fuss. You'll order your pint. Whoever is behind the bar might engage with you or they might not. If they don't, you have a lovely quiet pint. If they do, they might ask where you're from. This can turn into a great chat, usually dictated by finding some commonality in that distinctly Irish way. It's not about finding out that you both like jigsaws or watched *The Sopranos*. It's about them having been to where you're from and maybe having a connection. Maybe they have a cousin who lives nearby – do you know them? Or maybe it's you telling them who you know locally or that you went to the Gaeltacht down the road 20 years ago and perhaps they know your *bean an tí*? This could just as easily happen with a local sitting at the bar. It can be a short chat or it could turn into a few pints. Either way, there is something so wholesome about it that makes you feel like the Ireland we sell, the land of *céad míle fáilte*, is still alive and well.

Impressing tourists

The other side of this is striking up a chat with visiting tourists. The real kind, the ones not from Ireland. You'll spot them because they probably have proper rain gear and hiking boots (us Irish always seem to dress for the weather we want, not the weather we get). They'll turn to you as they sip their half pints and say, 'Are you local?' They won't know the difference between Kerry and Kilkenny anyway, you hope, so you reply, 'Sure, aren't we all?'

They probably want to know when the rain will stop or the best way to get to somewhere. Whatever it is, you're in. They buy you a pint. Here's your chance to show off your expertise in simply being Irish. It's a great buzz. They might tell you about their great-great-grand uncle who grew up over the road, are you related? Or you might impress them with your *cúpla focal as Gaeilge*. It's a win-win here. They've had a proper chat with a 'local' and you've got to feel like some sort of savant simply by opening your mouth.

Showing off to tourists

You have a friend in town. You know they are going to expect at least one pint that encapsulates what they think having a pint in Ireland should be. Luckily for you, there are a plethora of pubs to choose from in most towns and cities. But you can't pick just any pub, even though it would probably do the trick. You need to pick a pub that lets you show off the patriotism that arises from taking an out-of-towner for a scoop.

Anything old or Victorian will do the job (see also 'Victorian pints'), as will anything that is part of a literary tour or any pub you have a vague historical story about. You walk into a pub you've likely been to many times before and your tour guide switch turns on. You become an expert on the pints and crisps – the same pints and crisps they have in pretty much every pub in the country. You insist they must try Scampi Fries with the pints – Irish tapas! (See also 'Crisps and pints') You remember some historical facts about the pub and maybe launch into an explanation of the 1916 Rising that you only half remember, hoping the barman can't hear your half-arsed attempt at a story. Or you nod and point at the picture of James Joyce on the wall and regale them with your hotchpotch version of *Ulysses* (see also 'Pints, pubs and poets').

Your out-of-towner goes home suitably impressed and you realise you must brush up on your Irish history for the next visit.

UNPLANNED PINTS

Unplanned pints are a special thing. You're out for a walk or you're on your way home from work and someone says, 'Pint?'

It's unexpectedly warm and sunny in May and you walk past a beer garden. Pint?

You have an afternoon free and you bump into a friend in town. Pint?

You've no plans on a Friday and are sitting at home contemplating watching *The Late Late* when a text comes in. Pint?

Whatever the set-up, it's the impromptu nature, the sheer spontaneity that makes a random pint a bit more magical than the ones you've spent weeks planning. You forget about having dinner or that your work laptop is in your bag or that you have to get up early the next day and just settle into the moment. Cheers to that.

VICTORIAN PINTS

In his book *Three Castles Burning*, Donal Fallon writes, 'The age of Victoria – which spanned a reign of sixty-three years on the throne (1837–1901) – transformed these islands. Dublin and Ireland were transformed by the changes in architecture, infrastructure, science, politics and more besides.'

'And more besides' includes the exquisite Victorian pubs of Dublin – pubs that we still frequent nearly 200 years later and that still pour some of the finest pints going.

There are fewer than 20 authentic Victorian pubs left in Dublin. To walk into one of them is to walk into another era. Most retain their original fixtures, fittings and Victorian characteristics. It all adds up to a unique, old-fashioned ambience. Leaving one after a few hours, you could almost imagine walking out onto cobblestone streets with the horse-drawn carriages of the time.

VICTORIAN PUBS IN DUBLIN

Bowe's	International Bar	Ryan's of
Cassidy's	Kehoe's	Parkgate Street
Doheny & Nesbitt	The Long Hall	Slattery's
Finnegan's of Dalkey	The Norseman	The Stag's Head
Gaffney's	O'Neill's	The Swan
The Hut	The Palace Bar	Toners

THE VOCABULARY OF PINTS

'Any *craic*? It looks like high-stool weather. Will we stall down for a couple? I have an awful goo on me' might be gibberish to any non-Irish readers, but to most of us it basically means, 'It's raining, let's go to the pub. I'm thirsty!'

While Ireland may be a predominantly English-speaking country, the English we speak here is very much our own. Hiberno-English (or Anglo-Irish) is full of colloquial words and sayings that are commonplace to us. Many of them are direct translations of our own Irish language or iterations of Irish words we once used.

Craic is one of the best-known words. You can't talk about pubs and pints and not mention the *craic*. Confused tourists take a minute to realise we're not talking about hard drugs. *Craic* can mean anything that involves fun, devilment or merriment, but it has lots of other uses too.

High-stool weather basically just means it's raining (i.e. pub weather).

Stall down means the same thing as *head down* or *go down*. It's also used in 'stall the ball', which means to wait.

We talk about going for a *couple of pints*, but in Ireland a couple doesn't mean two. It can mean anything from two up to ten, really. It's subjective. So when someone says, 'Will we go for a couple of pints?', don't assume you're having an early night.

An awful goo means you're thirsty for a drink.

PINT OF PLAIN

PINT OF PAIN

COLLECTIVE TERMS FOR PINTS

A feed of pints	A few quick ones	A game of pints
A few cheeky Gs	A few scoops	A *geansaí* load
A few cold ones	A few sneaky ones	A hape of pints
A few delectables	A few steals	A pull
A few jars	A few sups	A rake of pints
A few pints		A wheen of pints

NAMES FOR PINTS

Black cow's milk	Heavies	Roaster
Britney	Holy water	Scoop
Choc ice	Jar	Settler
Cold one	Juice	Sharpener
Creamer	Livener	Slug
Creamy dreamy	Morning porter	Soup/bowl of soup
Dark one	One	Steal
Dasheen	Pint of black	Swiftie
Froths	Pint of plain	The cure
Frothy one	Pint of the black stuff	Vitamin G
Gargle	*Pinteen*	Vitamin water
Gat	Porter	Wan
Gravy	Refresher	Whipper

ACT OF GOING FOR PINTS

Go for a stroll	On the lash	On the tear
Go for a sup	On the sauce	On the town
On the gargle		Out on the town

SLANG FOR BEING DRUNK

Addled	Half-cut	Roasted
Ar meisce	Hammered	Rotten
Baloobas	In a hoop	Ruined
Bananas	Intoxicated	Sauced
Banjoed	Jarred	Scuttered
Binned	Langered	Seeing double
Blathered	Legless	Shit-faced
Blind	Locked	Sloppy
Blotto	Messy	Sloshed
Bolloxed	Mouldy	Smashed
Boozed up	Muddled	Snookered
Buckled	*Ólta*	Soused
Car parked	Ossified	Stocious
Cut	Paralytic	Three sheets to the wind
Destroyed	Pickled	
Drunk	Pissed	Tipsy
Flute-ered	Plastered	Trolleyed
Fuddled	Polluted	Twisted
Gee-eyed	Rat-arsed	Wasted
Had a skinful	Rat-faced	Wrote off

WEDDING PINTS

The Irish wedding is a unique experience, and much like our pubs, they have a reputation for good times.

Pre-ceremony pints

It's often standard for the bride or groom to head for a pint with their entourage before the wedding ceremony, grooms in particular. We've all seen it: the groom looking suitably nervous and uncomfortable in his three-piece suit, sweat building on his brow. There may be a cheer when he enters a pub as the locals spot a groom-to-be or at least nods and well wishes from any other punters. A worried brother or groomsman will be watching the clock and fussing over pocket handkerchiefs or fixing ties and buttonholes.

Wedding guests will also often nip in on the way to the ceremony, looking forward to an early pint, especially if there's a mass to get through. The wedding groups are easy to spot. It's probably lunchtime or before and they are dressed to the nines, looking glam or uncomfortable but party-ready, perhaps sporting the notable Irish wedding guest uniform of blue suits and brown shoes, bright dresses and spindly high heels and a pile of clutch bags on the pub table.

The groom may have to head off but some savvy guests figure the bride will be at least another 15 minutes: 'Will we get another quick pint?' These are likely to be the good-time guests who will start the sing-song or attempt to Riverdance later.

The photo op pints

These days it's not uncommon for photographers to have 'couple drinking pints' in their shot list. A candid photo of the happy pair, married at last, saying '*Sláinte!*' and taking a glug of Guinness to mark the occasion. It's not always candid to take, though. Someone has to fetch the Guinness, most likely a shivering bridesmaid with inappropriate shoes on. I always lament those poor pints and hope they get drunk. Meanwhile...

Post-ceremony pints and pints before dinner

If there is even a whiff of a decent pub within a short distance of the ceremony or on the way to the afters, wedding guests will find it. The happy couple will have to head off with their wedding party for the obligatory photo shoot, so it's the perfect time for guests to sneak in another pint or two and catch up with friends and family. So far, so wholesome.

When you arrive at the venue, there is usually some sort of drinks reception. These days it's often some form of bubbles or a cocktail. But look past the clinking glasses and you'll no doubt find another cohort at the bar, seeking out a pint. It's a distinctly Irish wedding moment: everyone dressed up, sipping pints, delighted with life, ready for celebrations and carousing.

Dinner and afters

Next, there's usually a sit-down dinner. Beef or salmon? Pints will be brought to the table, especially by people who swear they aren't drinking the wine provided: 'It doesn't agree with me.' 'I'll be locked.' But invariably it gets drunk anyway.

There will be heartfelt or awkward speeches (usually a bit of both), toasts, cheers and betting about the length of the speech. The dance floor appears, the first dance, napkins in the air, the wedding cake. Pints.

There will be dodgy dancing, maybe some jiving, probably a sweaty dance to an old dance track. Heels are discarded in favour of bare feet or flip-flops. Someone will have fallen over by now. Then the Riverdance will happen, ties on heads and sing-songs. You'll be hoarse in the morning.

Anyone who hasn't skulked off to bed at this stage will be looking for the lock-in or residents' bar. These are form-building pints. You will remember lyrics to songs you didn't realise you knew. Christy Moore and Mary Black reign supreme. Pints are ordered and forgotten about just as quickly. Time for bed.

I DO

THINK WE HAVE ENOUGH TIME FOR ONE MORE

WEIGHTS AND MEASURES

When did a pint become a pint? Here we are talking about the physical pint – the actual volume of a pint. Perhaps not a huge contribution to the cultural background of the pint, but some of it may come in handy for a pub quiz one day...

When we talk about a pint, we talk about the imperial pint, which is 568ml.

The pint as we know it was introduced to Ireland during the 19th century. Prior to this, various regional systems were in use that often had their own units for liquid volume, which could differ from one locality to another. Firkin, leck and gill were a few of them.

Firkin This varied in size depending on the region but was usually a small cask or container. A firkin was typically smaller than a barrel and larger than a keg.

....

Leck The leck was a local unit of liquid measurement used in parts of Ireland. The exact size of a leck varied but it typically referred to a small container used for measuring liquids like milk or ale.

....

Gill In 19th-century Ireland, a pint was four gills.

Then along came the Weights and Measures Act of 1824. It established a uniform system of measurement throughout the United Kingdom, which included Ireland at the time. This act defined the imperial units of measurement, including the pint, based on the British system. The British imperial pint, which is equal to 20 fluid ounces or approximately 568 millilitres, became the standardised measurement for liquids, including beer and other beverages.

A FEW PINTS

The pint glass in Ireland was included in the Legal Metrology as part of the liquid measures of capacity that were legalised in the Weights and Measures (General) Regulations, 1928.

The pint measurement was nearly changed back in the 1990s when the EU wanted Ireland and the UK to adopt the metric system by 1 January 1995. But neither government was happy about changing the pint. They successfully sought a derogation and by 2008 the European Parliament agreed on an indefinite opt-out to allow the continued use of the pint for draught beer, cider and bottled milk.

....

Whatever your views on his politics, William of Orange did one good thing for Ireland: he gave us a fair pint measure, writes Cian Molloy in *The Story of the Irish Pub*:

❝ William of Orange also deserves commemoration by Irish drinkers for giving us fair measure, for it is he who introduced the legal requirement that all pint vessels in pubs bear an assay mark, certifying that they could hold a full pint measure.

....

WELL-EARNED PINTS

Well-earned indicates that something is deserved, but hard work, working hard, hardly working – it's subjective.

The actual well-earned pint

The epitome of the actual well-earned pint is the after-work pint (see also pages 9–12) but it's also applicable to any domestic work or chores like DIY, gardening or assembling flatpack furniture – anything physical, anything taxing and usually not voluntary.

The well-earned pints we tell ourselves are well-earned

These are the pints we feel we deserve after we've done something taxing but it's often something completely voluntary or something we do for fun.

Post-sports A popular route to the well-earned pint. Playing in a match, a round of golf, maybe some tennis. Sometimes even watching sport qualifies (see also 'Sports and pints').

....

Post-outdoors Hiking, walking, running, sea swimming, you name it.

....

Post-shopping The bags are heavy and your feet are sore. A pint is needed. Technically, shopping can also fall under the actual well-deserved pints category, particularly at Christmas (see also 'Christmas pints').

....

Miscellaneous Making that phone call you've been putting off. Booking that flight. Dropping something you borrowed back to the person you borrowed it from. They could all potentially earn you a pint.

WOMEN, PUBS AND PINTS

Did you know that women were the original brewers and beer drinkers? To be fair, I didn't know until I read Mallory O'Meara's book *Girly Drinks: A World History of Women and Alcohol*. She goes right back to 7000 BCE in Mesopotamia and the city of Sumer, where she tells us life as a woman was pretty good, and one industry where women ruled was brewing. She writes, 'Beer, at the very beginning of its history, was a girl thing.'

❝ One of the earliest known depictions of a person drinking is an approximately 25,000-year-old carving, chiselled into a cliff at Laussel in the Dordogne region of France. This carving depicts a nude woman, with one hand on her belly, and holding what looks like a drinking horn in the other. Some male historians posit that it is not a drinking horn but rather some kind of musical instrument that the woman is holding incorrectly. Imagine being so staunch in your belief that women aren't drinkers that you think someone would take the time to immortalize a picture of the world's worst hornblower into the side of a cliff. Either way, she's called the Venus of Laussel, she's great, and she is very likely the earliest surviving artistic representation of drinking.

Women brewed and drank a lot of beer, and when they drank they toasted not to a god, but to a goddess called Ninkasi. The first large-scale brewers were the priestesses of Ninkasi. The women who worked in the temples were paid in beer. Taverns were female owned and operated. Booze became more than a part of the diet – it became part of the culture, religion and society, all under the watchful eyes of the women brewing and drinking it. O'Meara writes:

> **❝** The foundations of alcohol craft and culture were laid by female hands. The first known depiction of drinking was of a woman, and the first alcohol-related deity was a goddess. Thousands of years before Christians drank the wine of Eucharist, thousands of years before Dionysus was worshipped with wine in Greece, Ninkasi was honored with beer by the Sumerian women who brewed and drank it. Her dominion over all aspects of alcohol is a symbol of how influential women have been.

So the next time you or anyone in your presence thinks that beer is not a woman's domain, think again.

Women in pubs

Much as I love an old man's pub (see also pages 130–1), as a feminist, I wonder if I should have an issue with calling them 'old man's pubs'. And not only calling them that, but seeking them out, putting them on a pedestal, sending people to them and writing a book about them?

Well, the thing is, the old pubs – those traditional pubs we love – they are men's pubs. They were built for men. Women were an afterthought, much like the hastily added ladies' toilets many of them still have. You know the type, a pokey loo in a hidden corner or a draughty spot down a long corridor.

> **❝** If you want to know how a society treats its women, all you have to do is look into the bottom of a glass. For thousands of years, raising a toast as a woman was a subversive act. In many places all over the world, it still is. But if they get paid less, withstand more pain and have to fight against more oppression, aren't women more deserving of a goddamn drink? **(O'Meara, 2022)**

For a long time, Irish pubs were predominantly the preserve of men. Many books exploring the subject claim it was a place for men to gather, to drink, to socialise, to discuss business and politics and to escape the responsibilities of their daily lives. The poor creatures. Women belonged in the house, in the domestic sphere. They did their drinking at home, sending someone else, maybe a son, to the pub to fetch a jug of porter.

By the 1960s women started to get a look in, but only in progressive pubs and for the most part they would still have had to sit out of sight in a snug (see also 'Snugs'). As late as the 1970s, it was still uncommon to see women in pubs. Some places might let a woman in if she was accompanied by a man. But even then women weren't supposed to be served pints of beer, and if they were, they might be instructed to pour it into two half-pint glasses (see also 'Half pints').

Shockingly, it did not become illegal for a pub to refuse to serve a woman because of her sex until the Equal Status Act was passed in 2000.

If women were allowed in, they were not expected to sit with the men. Many of our pubs still have a layout that reflect this, with a bar space (that was meant for men) and a lounge space (that was meant for women).

There were exceptions, of course. In Donal Fallon's brilliant podcast Three Castles Burning, he has an episode called 'Grogan's: The making of a literary pub'. In it, he gives an insight into how women were viewed in Dublin pubs in these decades:

❝ The pub attracted many women, including Kathleen Behan, who mingled among its clientele. In 1972, when Terry Kelleher published *The Essential Dublin*, he noted, 'No pubs are barred to women. There is an unstated convention that women use the lounge bar if there is one.' This division did not broadly apply in Grogan's, reflective of the kind of women drawn to the establishment. It's something we can easily overlook today – just how unique the equal standing of men and women within a public house was. Within Kearn's *Oral History of Dublin Pubs*, he notes rightly that during the 1960s and 1970s, segregated pubs toppled like dominoes but there were still exceptions. Tom Ryan, head barman of Stoneybatter institution Walshes for five decades, refused to seat women at the bar into the late 1980s, insisting that it was a male preserve. 'Men prefer to be on their own. I know this from experience. Women just wouldn't fit in.'

In the same episode, he talks to Dara Gannon, a Grogan's local and an author and photographer who produced a piece for the magazine *Stranger's Guide* on Grogan's. The equality of men and women in Grogan's pub was something he wished to emphasise to Donal:

❝ The pubs had changed probably in the sixties – men could bring their wives into the lounge bar, but here was a bar, a real bar, that would allow a woman to come in and drink by herself and meet her friends and again the bar staff and the owners were very protective of that. They were very much, we want a diverse bunch of people drinking here, and you know, strange as it may seem, that diversity began by allowing women to just drink at their own pace, at their own time.

Around the corner from Grogan's was another well-regarded pub with literary connections, Neary's, where Patrick Kavanagh and Brendan Behan are said to have drunk. But there was a much different attitude to women at the time in Neary's, highlighted by the brilliant Irish journalist, playwright and civil rights campaigner Nell McCafferty. In the early 1970s, she, along with 30 women, headed into Neary's pub just off Grafton Street. They each ordered a brandy, then once that was done, they dared

JUST THE 30 BRANDIES, PLEASE

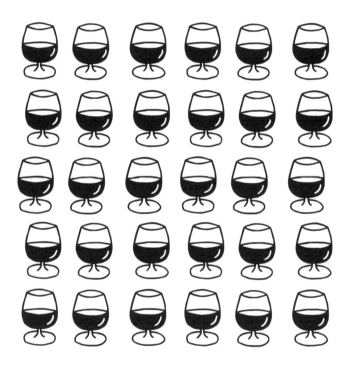

DON'T WORRY WE'LL GET YOU AT THE END

to order a single pint of Guinness. The bartender refused to serve the pint, so the women drank the brandies and walked out without paying. Afterwards, McCafferty said, 'He refused to serve, we refused to pay.'

These days pubs are mostly shared, democratic spaces. It's rare to find a pub in Ireland now with distinct divisions of men and women, although they do still exist. At a discussion I hosted about pubs and pints while researching this book, some members of the audience mentioned a pub in Waterford (they didn't name names) where there is still an unstated rule that women do not go into the bar. But it's only a matter of time before these last men-only spaces are infiltrated. Let's be honest – what publican wants to turn away a paying customer these days?

In addition, the current obsession with pints, with Guinness and with the 'aesthetic' of an old man's pub must mean that there are only rare corners and bars that have not yet been discovered by the next generation of all-gender pint drinkers looking for that perfect pint for their next Instagram post or TikTok video asking, 'Is this the best pint of Guinness in Ireland?'

It's taken years, but I don't let the pub stare-down intimidate me anymore. Now I will nod knowingly. It's a sign of an old man's pub, a proper pint, no fuss. I will order my pint and let them stare. I'll take a picture for the gram and raise a (pint) glass to Nell.

X AND INSTAGRAM: SOCIAL MEDIA PINTS

I was flummoxed as to what would be the X in the A to Z of Irish pints. X doesn't lend itself to many pint-related words – perhaps because there is no X in the Irish language alphabet? (There is also no j, k, q, v, w, y or z!) Then Elon Musk took over Twitter and changed it to X.

Pints and social media? I hear you say. Get away outta that, would ya? But there's no getting away from the fact that social media has shaped, and will continue to shape, our lives. Pints are no different.

You see, we love to debate, discuss and argue about pints. The price, the pour, the glass, the beer, the pub. While traditionally this has happened in the pub, or maybe on Joe Duffy, these days you're just as likely – in fact, maybe even more likely – to come across heated pint discussions on social media.

Posting your receipt

Twitter (sorry, X), Instagram and Facebook have all become fertile ground for venting about the price of pints (see also pages 152–3). Did you even have a pint in Temple Bar if you didn't take a picture of the receipt and post it in outrage on your socials?

Shit London Guinness

You can't talk about pints on social media and not mention Shit London Guinness, an Instagram account set up by Irishman Ian Ryan to document exactly that - shit pints of Guinness in London (see also 'Bad pints' for more on this). You might think that an account that posts pictures of shit pints would worry Guinness, but no. If anything, I'd say the phenomenon that is Shit London Guinness has to be part of Guinness's surge in popularity in the UK over the last while. That old adage that 'all publicity is good publicity' seems to ring true.

The more shitty pictures Ryan posted, the more we discussed not just what was wrong with those pints but also what made a good pint, a perfect pint. We started posting our own: look at mine! Ryan set up another account called Beautiful Pints to pay homage to all the photos of great pints he was getting tagged in but it will never garner the same amount of engagement as the original Shit London Guinness. It's just not as fun.

Posting perfect pints

Guinness continues to be the darling of the small screen, whether it's shit pints or beautiful pints. It makes sense. After decades of mythical marketing and an unshakable heritage, Guinness has brand loyalty others can only dream of. Add to that the fact that the product is aesthetically pleasing and it's no wonder modern socials are awash with pints of the black stuff.

Posting a pint of stout seems to have a particular meaning on social media. It says, Look at me, I'm having a civilised drink. I'm having a grown-up chat with a pal, I'm looking after myself, #selfcare, etc. A nice pint of stout doesn't scream, I'm going on the piss! Posting a vodka and Coke doesn't have quite the same effect.

Even posting other beers doesn't get the same kind of love and adoration a pint of stout does. Stout reigns supreme as the acceptable drink to show off about, and not just Guinness. Murphy's and of course a Creamy Beamy do the job just as well.

PERFECT

Writing about this in *Vittles*, Anna Kinsella says:

> " I was reminded of this image recently when Guinness discourse started floating around, all started by a tweet that questioned whether those who have aesthetic opinions on Guinness have been brainwormed by 'commodity fetishism'; that these opinions were nothing more than brand specifications and marketing, parroted by drinkers who have succumbed to decades of successful advertising. It would have been easy to create a second brain-expanding image from the debate this generated about whether it's ever okay to have aesthetic preferences about your pint, from no (it's anti-worker) to yes (the proletariat deserve the treat of a properly poured head) to no (there's no difference anyway) to yes (things were better when Guinness used to inspect the pubs who served their pints and now the world's gone to pot) to no (this is a pro-cop position and you are arguing for the continued existence of the Guinness Stasi) to death. **(Kinsella, 2023)**

Splitting the G

Social media loves a challenge. Remember the one that started it all, the ice bucket challenge? These days there is a much more pleasant pint-based challenge called splitting the G.

For this, you need a well-poured pint of Guinness in a proper Guinness glass: a tulip-shaped one with the Guinness name printed on it. The challenge is to take just the right amount of your first gulp of Guinness so that when you sit the pint back down, the remaining stout is level with the middle of the G in the word Guinness.

Before we heard of splitting the G, there was another 'right' way to take your first sip. According to the website Ladbible, 'The "split the G" crowd faces stiff competition from the people who reckon the right way to pull off the Guinness Challenge is to drink until your line is between the top of the G and the bottom of the harp.'

Technically, splitting the G is probably harder. You have to be that bit more precise. But the thing is, it has a catchy name. Social media loves that too, so for now, until something new comes along, splitting the G is where it's at.

The tilt test
Sometimes also referred to as the 'cream test', this is a popular way of 'checking' that your Guinness (or any other stout, I'm sure) is good. When your pint is settled, you gently tilt the glass to see if the head retains its shape and rises above the lip of the glass. It's become one of the ways to show off your perfect pint on socials. Just take a look at the #titltest hashtag on any of the social channels for a glimpse of how much people love to do this.

Guinness, on the ball as always, even released an advertising campaign in 2023 that features the tilt. The ad, which also appears on beer mats, simply says 'LOVELY DAY FOR A' and then features a perfect pint being tilted with a blue sky background.

THE ZOO AND PINTS

Would you choose the zoo over the pub? That's exactly what social reformers hoped for in the 1840s when Dublin Zoo was opened on a Sunday 'after morning Church services in an attempt to divert people from attending public houses', writes Kevin Martin in his account of the history of the Irish pub, *Have Ye No Homes to Go To?*

He documents a discussion in the House of Commons where James Haughton, 'a prominent social reformer and temperance campaigner', argued that opening other places of amusement on Sunday might stop folks from heading to the pub. Spoiler alert: it didn't.

The zoo popped up again when I came across a blog post on Publin.ie entitled 'When Patrick Kavanagh got a pint in the Zoo on Good Friday'. The post is about Anthony Cronin's book *Dead as Doornails*, a recollection of Cronin's relationship with some of Ireland's literary giants from the 1950s to the 1970s. Cronin recounts a story about Patrick Kavanagh, who was fond of drink, and his quest for a pint one Good Friday (see also 'Ecumenical pints').

     “ Kavanagh happened to bump into 'The Pope' O'Mahoney, a barrister and political satirist, who was a member of the Zoological Society. Apparently, as a member, O'Mahony could gain access to the members restaurant in Dublin Zoo, where drink was served, even on Good Friday. And so, off they went to have a pint in the Zoo.

Lions and tigers and pints. Who knew?

BIBLIOGRAPHY

Amis, Kingsley, *On Drink* (Jonathan Cape, 1972).

Bohan, Eddie, *Thirst for Freedom: Alcohol and the Battle for Irish Independence* (Kilmainham Tales Teo, 2020).

Carrigy, Aoife, 'A place apart, in its own time: The Irish pub as portrayed in John McGahern's short stories', *Journal of Franco-Irish Studies*, 5/1 (2019).

Connolly, Robert E., *The Rise and Fall of the Irish Pub* (Liffey Press, 2010).

Downing, John, 'That's Bass: The intertwined history of a pale ale, politics, boycotts and Brexit', *Irish Independent*, 14 September 2021.

Doyle, Roddy, *The Van* (Viking, 1992).

Dunworth, Ali, 'Another round? How to save our pubs', *Sunday Times Ireland*, 28 January 2024.

Fallon, Donal, *Three Castles Burning: A History of Dublin in Twelve Streets* (New Island, 2022).

Fennell, James and Bunbury, Turtle, *The Irish Pub* (Thames & Hudson, 2008).

Gluckman, David, *That S*it Will Never Sell!: A Book About Ideas by the Person Who Had Them* (Prideaux Press, 2022).

Goodman, Conor, 'The 10 best Irish pubs in the world (outside Ireland)', *Irish Times*, 15 March 2015.

Irish Times, 'Traditional bar culture gives way to bustling super-pub scene', 31 August 1998.

Kearns, Kevin C., *Dublin Pub Life and Lore: An Oral History* (Gill & Macmillan, 1996).

Killen, John, *The Pure Drop: A Book of Irish Drinking* (Blackstaff Press, 1987).

Kinsella, Anna, 'Nine ways of looking at a pint of Guinness', *Vittles Magazine*, 30 January 2023.

Macmanus, Annie, 'I felt an ache. I was homesick for Ireland', *Irish Times*, 19 December 2020.

Maloney, Bridget, 'An ode to the sesh: A very short history of a beloved tradition', *Trinity News*, 16 September 2018.

Martin, Kevin, *Have Ye No Homes to Go To?: The History of the Irish Pub* (Collins Press, 2016).

McGarry, Dr Marion, *Irish Customs and Rituals* (Orpen Press, 2020).

McGarry, Dr Marion, 'Is it last orders for the Irish pub?', *RTÉ Brainstorm*, 25 August 2023.

McKenna, John and McKenna, Sally, *Milk: The Story of Ireland's Culinary Treasure* (Estragon Press, 2020).

Molloy, Cian, *The Story of the Irish Pub* (Liffey Press, 2002).

Mullally, Una, 'New York's new Irish bars', *Irish Times*, 11 February 2023.

Ó Drisceoil, Diarmuid and Ó Drisceoil, Donal, *The Murphy's Story: The History of Lady's Well Brewery, Cork* (Murphy Brewery Ltd, 1997).

O'Meara, Mallory, *Girly Drinks: A World History of Women and Alcohol* (Hurst, 2022).

Pubs. Pints. People podcast, 'Diving into the history of CAMRA', Season 1, Episode 10, 16 June 2020.

Ryan, Ian, *A Beautiful Pint: One Man's Search for the Perfect Pint of Guinness* (Bloomsbury, 2023).

ACKNOWLEDGEMENTS

The next time you find yourself contemplating, 'Will I go for that pint?', just know that it was over unplanned pints that this book was dreamed up. If I hadn't been seeking out a Guinness at a posh party, I wouldn't have delivered an enthusiastic monologue to Kristin Jensen about how pints are the best and perhaps Kristin might not have shut me up by saying, 'There's a book in this!' So huge thank you to Kristin, my publisher and editor, for taking a chance on both me and this book.

Thank you to Hephee for creating picture-perfect drawings to go alongside my musings and to Graham Threw and Laura Merrigan for making it all look so smart. Thank you to Emma Marijewycz and Olivia Collins for getting the word out about the book.

Thank you to the many professional pint experts who helped me with my research and gave me brilliant insights and quotes, especially Donal Fallon, Judith Boyle and in the Guinness archive, Eibllin Colgan. Big thanks to Neil Cotter, who gave me invaluable sporting expertise – I owe you a pint (or three).

I joke that I've been researching this for over 20 years but I really have. From Maynooth to Dublin and Dingle to Greece, London and Australia, every pint I've drunk, every chat I've had and every pub I've been in has contributed, so a huge *go raibh maith agat* to everyone who's had a pint with me. If you can see yourselves in sections of this book, then I know I've done my job.

TOGETHER

FOREVER

A special thanks to the pint partners I've had from the early days. You know who you are and I know I'm lucky to still have many of you around for pints and support to this day.

The biggest *buíochais* of all goes to my family for their unwavering support.

Finally, this book wouldn't exist without Irish pubs, publicans and brilliant bar staff, so thank you all. I hope that my cataloguing of Irish pints like this captures even an ounce of the magic that you all provide for us.

Sláinte!

ABOUT THE AUTHOR

Ali Dunworth is a writer, journalist, consultant and events curator who loves writing and talking about food and drink so much that she's made a career out of it. She started out working in hospitality before a career behind the scenes in food TV. In between TV productions, she always returned to bar and restaurant work, either waiting tables, making drinks or back in the kitchen. There was even a year spent cooking at Lord's Cricket Ground and another running butchers in Melbourne. As a freelance food, drink and travel writer, Ali contributes to the *Irish Times*, *Food & Wine Magazine* and many others. She also curates and hosts numerous Irish food events and festival stages. At the heart of everything Ali does is great local food and drink and a hunger for the stories that go with them. Cooking, writing, storytelling, washing up, pouring pints, writing about pints – she's done them all, and as a freelancer, she's always prepared to do any of them again.

@alidunworth

ABOUT THE ILLUSTRATOR

Stephen Heffernan is a designer and illustrator who is best known for his work on Instagram under the name Hephee (pronounced heff-ee). His work has a largely comedic focus and is based around social commentary and the nuances of everyday life. After working in the design and ad industry for eight years, as of 2023 he has gone freelance, working on national and international projects with clients such as Coca-Cola, Jameson and An Post.

@hephee

Nine Bean Rows
23 Mountjoy Square
Dublin
D01 E0F8
Ireland
@9beanrowsbooks
ninebeanrowsbooks.com

First published 2024
Text copyright © Ali Dunworth, 2024
Illustrations copyright © Stephen Heffernan, 2024

ISBN: 978-1-7392105-8-8

Editor: Kristin Jensen
Illustrator: Stephen Heffernan
Design and layout: grahamthew.com
Printed by L&C Printing Group, Poland

The paper in this book is produced using pulp from managed forests.